TWAYNE'S GREAT EDUCATORS SERIES

Samuel Smith, Ph.D.
Editor

HORACE MANN
Champion of Public Schools

1

HORACE MANN

Horace Mann

Champion of Public Schools

ROBERT B. DOWNS

Twayne Publishers, Inc.   New York

Library of Congress Cataloging in Publication Data

Downs, Robert Bingham, 1903-
   Horace Mann: champion of public schools.

   (Twayne's great educators series)
   Bibliography: p.
   1.   Mann,   Horace,   1796-1859.   2.   Education—
Massachusetts—History. I. Title.
LB695.M35D68   370'.92'4 [B]   73-14831
ISBN 0-8057-3544-5

MANUFACTURED IN THE UNITED STATES OF AMERICA

Preface

My deep interest in Horace Mann began some years ago when I undertook to select twenty-five works which the evidence seemed to show had been most influential in American history. It soon became crystal clear that Horace Mann's notable series of *Annual Reports,* written for the Massachusetts Board of Education from 1837 to 1848, merited inclusion in the group eventually included in my *Books That Changed America* (N. Y.: Macmillan, 1970).

The impact of Horace Mann's ideas and achievements has been profoundly felt in the educational world at home and abroad for well over a century. Few figures in our history have made such a pervasive and enduring impression on American culture and civilization. Many of the issues raised by Mann are as live and relevant today as they were in the eighteen-forties, when he was a highly effective missionary for universal public education. Nothing could have been more appropriate, therefore, than Horace Mann's election in 1900 to the Hall of Fame, one of the first names to be thus immortalized.

Accordingly, when Dr. Samuel Smith, editor in chief of Twayne Publishers' "Great Educators Series," invited me to contribute a biography of Horace Mann, I accepted with alacrity and satisfaction. The body of writings on Mann, much of it specialized in nature, is enormous, as is revealed in several published bibliographies. The question may legitimately be asked, therefore, whether another life is needed. As justification, it should be noted that the emphasis in the present work is on Mann's educational philosophy and theories and their widespread influence, instead of on his personal affairs, the focus of most biographical treatments. Mann's pertinence for the twentieth century lies in his ideas and ideals.

Acknowledgment should be made to Elizabeth C. Downs for her assistance in research and to Clarabelle Gunning and Deloris Holiman for the preparation of the manuscript of this work.

Robert B. Downs

Contents

Chronology

1796 Born May 4, at Franklin, Massachusetts. One of five children of Thomas and Rebecca (Stanley) Mann.

1809 Death of father.

1816 Entered Brown University as sophomore, after intensive preparation under Samuel John Barrett, brilliant itinerant teacher.

1819 Graduated with high honors from Brown University. Entered law office of J. J. Fiske, Wrentham, Massachusetts, for few months, and then returned to Brown as tutor in Latin and Greek.

1821 Resigned from Brown to study law under Judge James Gould at Litchfield, Connecticut, where he made brilliant record.

1823 Admitted to Massachusetts bar; entered law office of James Richardson in Dedham, Massachusetts, and continued successful practice of law for fourteen years.

1824 Began active interest in public affairs.

1827- Elected member of Massachusetts General Court (legisla-
1833 ture).

1830 Married to Charlotte Messer, daughter of President of Brown University; wife died in 1832, less than two years later.

1833 Moved to Boston to continue law practice.

1833- Elected member of Massachusetts Senate.
1837

1835- Senate President. Instrumental in establishing Mas-
1837 sachusetts State Hospital for the Insane.

1837 Resigned from legislature to accept appointment as Secretary to the newly established Massachusetts Board of Education.

1837- Secretary, Massachusetts Board of Education.
1848

1839 Founded *The Common School Journal*, to inform and influence the public in Massachusetts.

1837-1848 Prepared and published a series of twelve highly influential *Annual Reports.*

1843 After marriage to Mary Peabody on May 1, traveled in Europe to observe educational systems of England, Ireland, Scotland, Holland, Belgium, France, Germany, and Switzerland.

1848 Resigned Secretaryship of Board of Education to fill vacancy in U.S. House of Representatives, created by death of John Quincy Adams; there Mann became a leader of the antislavery forces.

1852 Defeated as Free-Soil candidate for Governor of Massachusetts. Accepted Presidency of Antioch College, Yellow Springs, Ohio.

1859 Died, August 2, 1859, at Antioch.

1900 Elected to American Hall of Fame.

CHAPTER 1

Early Years

To find an explanation of Horace Mann's truly remarkable later career in public education, an examination of his early years is rewarding. As one often finds in analyses of the careers of great leaders, Mann was the right man in the right place at the right time, with exactly the qualities of mind, personality, and background required to meet his opportunities.

Horace Mann's ancestors came to New England near the middle of the seventeenth century. The precise date has been lost. Horace, one of five children, was born on a farm at Franklin, Massachusetts, May 4, 1796. The town had been named for Benjamin Franklin, who as a token of appreciation for the honor presented the community with a collection of books to found the oldest public library in America.

Horace's most vivid memories of his childhood were of hard work and constant church attendance. Work began at dawn and continued until night descended. Typically, there was never an end to the demands of the corn field, the hay field, the barnyard, and the kitchen garden. In winter, there were wood chopping and snow shoveling. Horace took little satisfaction in the unremitting toil.

Franklin itself was a well-organized community of farmers, undergoing rapid economic and social changes. The Mann farm, which had been handed down through several generations, was reasonably self-sufficient and prosperous. The field, the wood lot, the garden, and the orchard provided the family with essential raw materials. Wool and flax were processed for clothing and

nearly all essential food was grown on the farm. It was a hard way
of life, returning little more than a bare subsistence, but there was
also some sense of security for the individual members, each of
whom was expected to contribute his part and to receive the
rewards of his industry.

The life of the town of Franklin revolved around the meetinghouse. Nathanael Emmons, a recent Yale graduate, became the
minister in 1773 and remained in the position for more than half
a century, until 1827. Here, as a boy, Mann heard stern Puritan
doctrines preached and received impressions of the most rigid
Calvinism—a traumatic experience that remained with him
throughout his life. In later years, Mann recorded his memory of
the period:

More than by toil, or by the privation of any natural taste, was the inward
joy of my youth blighted by theological inculcations. The pastor of the
church in Franklin was the somewhat celebrated Dr. Emmons, who not
only preached to his people, but ruled them for more than fifty years. He
was an extra or hyper-Calvinist—a man of pure intellect, whose logic was
never softened in its severity by the infusion of any kindliness of sentiment. He expounded all the doctrines of total depravity, election, and
reprobation, and not only the eternity but the extremity of hell torments,
unflinchingly and in their most terrible significance, while he rarely if
ever descanted upon the joys of heaven, and never, to my recollection,
upon the essential and necessary happiness of a virtuous life. Going to
church on Sunday was a sort of religious ordinance in our family, and
during all my boyhood, I hardly ever remember of staying at home.[1]

To a sensitive lad such as Horace, constant exposure to this
type of sermon was frightening. The gloomy religious dogmas
"spread like a pall of blackness over the whole heavens, shutting
out every beautiful and glorified thing; while beyond that curtain
of darkness," night and day, he "could see the bottomless and
seething lake, filled with torments, and hear the wailings of its
victims." At the age of fourteen, Horace came to a final parting of
the ways with Emmons, when the latter in a sermon at the funeral
of Horace's brother Stephen preached on the damnation of those
dying unconverted. Henceforth, Mann noted, he "began to con-
struct the theory of Christian Ethics and doctrine respecting
virtue and vice, rewards and penalties, time and eternity, God
and His providence, which, with such modifications as advancing

age and a wider vision must impart, I still retain, and out of which my life has flowed." Especially strong was his desire to lead a life of public service. "All my boyish castles in the air," Mann wrote, "had reference to doing something for mankind."

Educational opportunities in Franklin were extremely limited. The Manns and their neighbors taxed themselves less than a hundred dollars a year for a schoolmaster's salary and to heat and maintain a one-room school building. During the winter term, the temperature was frigid, the only heat coming from an open fireplace. Mann later remarked humorously that the fact that there were numerous leaks in the roof was of small consequence and caused only momentary discomfort since the floor also leaked and kept the rain and melting snow from accumulating inside. The school year was short. According to Mann, until he was sixteen, he never had more than ten weeks of schooling in a year. Each child was supposed to be provided with a copy of the *New England Primer,* both for learning the alphabet and for moral instruction. Long sections of the *Westminster Assembly Shorter Catechism* had to be memorized and Dr. Emmons made regular visits to the classroom to question pupils on moral and doctrinal matters. Horace Mann was one of the brighter pupils; he recalled that by the age of ten he was "familiar with the whole creed, and knew all the arts of theological fence, by which objections to it were parried." On the last day of the school year, parents were invited for a closing "exhibition" of their children's progress, during which there were questions and answers, spelling bees, arithmetic drills, and memorized poetry and orations.

The qualifications of the teachers were on a par with the dilapidated school buildings. As Mann characterized them, "My teachers were very good people, but they were very poor teachers . . . with all our senses and our faculties glowing and receptive how little were we taught. . . Our eyes were never trained to distinguish forms and colors. Our ears were strangers to music. . . . Of all our faculties, the memory for words was the only one specially appealed to. . . . All ideas outside of the book were contraband articles, which the teacher confiscated or threw overboard."[2]

Another source for Mann's education was the books donated to the town by Benjamin Franklin. The books had been chosen by the Reverend Richard Price of London, whom Franklin had asked to select "a parochial library for the use of a society of intelligent, respectable farmers, such as our country people generally consist of." The shipment of 116 books was received in 1786. Mann described the collection as follows:

Though the library consisted of old histories and theologies, suited "perhaps" to the taste of the "conscript fathers" of the town, but miserably adapted to the "proscript" children, yet I wasted my youthful ardor upon its martial pages and learned to glory in war, which both reason and conscience have since taught me to consider almost universally a crime.[3]

Mann's particular favorite was a five-volume edition of Gordon's *Tacitus,* but it appears that he waded through the entire lot of sermons, lives of statesmen, constitutions, and laws. It was doubtless this early childhood experience which later inspired him to remark, "Had I the power, I would scatter libraries over the whole land, as the sower sows his wheat field."

Mann's devotion to education and learning was stimulated further by his parents. Of their inspiration he wrote:

They always spoke of learning and learned men with enthusiasm and a kind of reverence. I was taught to take care of the few books we had, as though there was something sacred about them. I never dog's-eared one in my life, nor profanely scribbled upon the title-pages, margin, or fly-leaf, and would as soon have stuck a pin through my flesh as through the pages of a book.[4]

When Horace was thirteen years of age, his father died of tuberculosis, throwing on the shoulders of his young sons, Stanley and Horace, the burden of cultivating and maintaining the family farm. The father had assumed that life in Franklin would continue virtually unchanged, as it had for decades. Neither Stanley nor Horace, however, were agriculturists at heart. Furthermore, the community was in a state of transition. Shortly before Horace was born, the straw-braiding industry was started in Franklin. The town's women learned the art of braiding straw into strands which could be used in making ladies' hats. By 1812, straw bonnets were being made in Franklin for sale in Boston, Providence, New York, and elsewhere. For the first time, the citizens had a ready source of cash income. The Manns were promptly drawn into the new industry. Throughout the winter and summer months, once the farm chores were finished, straw braiding was done. To Horace, every moment seemed to be spent in "sedentary occupations" and he remembered a childhood of constant labor. The normal freedom of youth was lost, and reading for pleasure was considered sinful idleness, a situation which left Horace with a feeling of bitterness. "I believe in the rugged nursing of toil," he wrote, "but she nursed me too much." For him, the farm had become not a center for security, rest, and congenial family living, but a place of restraint and arduous toil.

The escape route was obviously a college education and training in a profession. His mother's reluctant consent was gained by Horace after considerable persuasion. There remained, however, the problem of preparation. Latin, Greek, and mathematics were basic requirements for admission to Brown or other universities in the East. Salvation came in the form of an odd personality, Samuel Barrett, an alcoholic itinerant schoolmaster with a phenomenal memory. Barrett could recite Greek or Latin for hours without a text and he was thoroughly familiar with the grammatical rules of the classical languages. Under him, Mann read the Greek Testament, Cicero, Virgil, and other classical works. To fill the gap in mathematics, preparatory to coming up against the college entrance examinations, Horace walked four miles to Wrentham to study with the Reverend William Williams, pastor of the Baptist meetinghouse, who introduced him to Euclid's geometry.

Mann's choice for college was Brown University, which a dozen other Franklin boys had attended in recent years. Brown was also attractive for economic reasons; tuition, room, and board cost $100 per year or less. By the summer of 1816, Mann's tutors decided that he knew enough Latin, Greek, and geometry to meet the entrance requirements, and in September he set out for Providence, thirty miles to the south of Franklin.

Upon arrival on the Brown campus—a single building—Mann had to pass both oral and written examinations, personally conducted by President Messer. The regulation for admission read: "Upon examination of the President and tutors the candidate must read accurately, construe and parse Tully and the Greek

Testament, and Virgil; and shall be able to write true Latin in prose; and hath learned the rules of Prosody and Vulgar Arithmetic; and shall bring suitable testimony of a blameless life and conversation." Horace passed with flying colors, testimony of his strenuous studies and the excellence of his teachers. He was immediately admitted to the sophomore class. There were deficiencies for him to make up, but it was anticipated that he could keep pace with students who had entered Brown a year earlier.

Mann's initial course of college study included a continuation of his work in the classical languages and geometry and classes in geography, logic, and public speaking. The teaching, at best, was mediocre. With one exception, all the faculty were past middle age. Their procedure was described by Mann's biographer, Jonathan Messerli, as follows: "When teaching, each planted himself firmly in his armchair at the head of the class and heard recitations. Each expected his students to repeat the exact contents of the textbook, including even obvious printer's mistakes. The teaching of foreign languages was largely a mechanical translating and parsing. . .Even instruction in geography followed the same pattern."[5]

Brown University in Mann's time lacked the prestige of Harvard and Yale. Students were drawn principally from the middle and lower classes, the sons of merchants, mechanics, and farmers of nearby areas. The university suffered severe financial limitations. Nevertheless, under Asa Messer's presidency, which lasted from 1802 to 1826, it became a strong institution. The English department provided effective training in composition and oratory—Horace Mann's chief interests. Active literary societies furnished forums for lively debates and orations.

Mann became a member of the United Society of Brothers, one of the literary groups, and the records show that he appeared frequently on its programs, usually to discuss some political or economic subject. Among the titles of his papers which have been preserved are "Separation of Church and State," "Immigration," "Lessons of European Politics," "On Foreigners in the United States," and "American Genius." His orations advocated establishment of a national university and the study of mathematics, but condemned the reading of fiction and attempts to restrict the freedom of the press. The extant records of his borrowings from the library show a particular concern with history and poetry.

Despite entering Brown on an advanced level, Mann soon closed the gap and attained the highest rank in his class. One of his contemporaries stated that he never heard a student translate the Greek and Roman classics with greater facility, accuracy, and elegance. It is not surprising, therefore, that when Mann graduated from college in 1819, he was chosen valedictorian of his college class. His choice of a subject as college orator was indicative of his future career: "The Gradual Advancement of the Human Species in Dignity and Happiness," a kind of utopian vision of the potentialities of mankind, exhibiting faith in education as a prime tool in the "accelerating improvability of the race."

While a student at Brown, Mann was a welcome visitor in President Messer's home. There he first met the president's daughter Charlotte, who was only ten years of age when Mann graduated. Eleven years later, Charlotte became his first wife, but lived less than two years after their marriage, her death being one of the great tragedies in Mann's life.

Immediately after leaving Brown, Mann entered the law office of J. J. Fiske of Wrentham. He saw the legal profession as the most promising avenue for entrance into political and public life. According to the statutes and tradition, admission to the bar required a young aspirant to spend three years reading law in a lawyer's office. Mann's legal career was delayed for two years, however, when, a few months later, President Messer invited him to return to Brown as a tutor in Latin and Greek and librarian, at a salary of $375 per year.

Though he was successful as a teacher, Mann's long-range goal remained the field of law. In 1821 he left Brown to study at Litchfield, Connecticut, under Judge James Gould, a Yale graduate, who was operating what was reputedly the first American law school. The school had been established in 1775 by Tapping Reeve, Aaron Burr's brother-in-law, who continued his association with it until 1820, just prior to Mann's entry, when Gould assumed its direction. Graduates of the school compiled a remarkable record: vice-presidents of the United States, Supreme Court justices, numerous senators and representatives in Congress, cabinet officers, governors, and other high officials.

Gould was a demanding master, with an encyclopedic knowledge of the law, both of abstract legal principles and of precedents in which the principles had been applied in specific cases. His lectures dealt with such practical areas as "Fraudulent Conveyances," "Law of Contract," and "Action on Debt." He spoke from a written manuscript and students were expected to record his words verbatim in permanent notebooks, later to become basic documents in their law libraries. Each Saturday morning the class was quizzed by Gould's assistant on the previous week's lectures.

Extracurricular features of the Litchfield school were particularly appealing to and enjoyed by Mann. Two social and debating societies had been formed by the students for legal discussions. In addition, a "moot court" was held each Monday evening. Students argued typical hypothetical cases before a justice and court made up of fellow students. The decision was reviewed by Gould or another lawyer. Two students were assigned to argue each case. Mann soon became a star performer and in his second year was elected by his fellow students as attorney general.

Under Gould's direction, Mann gained a superior professional education. One of his classmates, Jessup Scott, remembered him as the best law student and the best-read scholar in the school. By June, 1823, he had completed his preparation and had decided to settle in Dedham, Massachusetts, to practice law. Mann began by entering the office of James Richardson a prominent local attorney, and by intensive study was admitted to the bar in December, 1823. Two years later, the Norfolk Bar Association recommended Mann's admission to practice before the Supreme Judicial Court. His legal apprenticeship was at last completed.

Competition was keen among Dedham's lawyers, who were equal in number to the town's clergymen and exceeded doctors by two. But Mann was aggressive and his practice grew. By the end of three years, he was averaging fifteen cases each session and his reputation for success was growing. A contemporary reported that during his fourteen years of legal practice, Mann won four out of five contested cases. His cases were prepared with meticulous care and he made it a rule never to accept a cause that he was not convinced was right and his client honest.

Financial success was beginning to come to Mann along with his high reputation at the bar. The town of Dedham grew rapidly and was beginning to attract a considerable amount of industry. As a result, Mann's legal practice was of increasing complexity. His office records reveal cases concerned with domestic relations, corporation lawsuits, boundary disputes, and the defense of criminals. Legal work for merchants and for legal firms in Boston was becoming an important aspect of his business. Real wealth, however, escaped him. He made the mistake of backing his brother Stanley in the purchase and operation of two manufacturing companies. Their failure, due to Stanley's mismanagement, not only swept away Horace's savings, but involved him heavily in debt for some years afterward.

After the death of his wife, Charlotte Messer, Mann moved to Boston in 1833. There an expanded world of opportunities began to open up for him.

CHAPTER 2

Massachusetts Legislator

Horace Mann's interest in public affairs began early. A year after his admission to the bar, in 1824, he delivered a Fourth of July oration, at Dedham, that attracted the attention of John Quincy Adams, who described it as "of splendid composition and lofty eloquence," and predicted a brilliant career for its author. Two years later, a eulogy of John Adams and Thomas Jefferson spread Mann's fame among a wider public.

With a reputation as an extraordinarily successful attorney and an able orator, Mann's entry into the political arena was a foregone conclusion. He was elected to the state House of Representatives in 1827, served six years in that body, and then transferred to the Senate for a four-year term, 1833-37. During his last two years in the upper house, he was elected president, a rapid rise for a comparatively youthful member.

As state representative and senator, Mann held views and opinions that were statesmanlike and socially oriented, not merely political. Several years later, in reviewing his legislative career, Mann wrote, "While engaged in political life, I took a view deeper than mere politics have ever reached." With the expansion of the Union and the addition of new states, he noted that "Massachusetts was rapidly losing her relative rank and power in the republic." It could maintain its ascendancy, in Mann's judgment, by the full utilization of its intellectual and inventive resources and development of its industrial power. These facts motivated many of Mann's actions in the legislature.

With his proclivity for controversial subjects, Mann chose as the theme of his first speech in the House of Representatives a defense of religious liberty. The state of Massachusetts, through the legislature and Supreme Court, had tended, over the years, to place all religious beliefs on a basis of full equality before the law, despite resistance from orthodox Congregationalists. The Unitarian movement was spreading rapidly and many formerly Congregational pulpits were being filled by Unitarian ministers. At the same time, the church properties and endowed funds, built up through gifts and bequests from orthodox members, were falling into the hands of these "heretics."

The legislative battle began with the receipt of a petition submitted by the First Religious Society of Blandford, Massachusetts, in June, 1827. The petitioners, a thoroughly orthodox group, untainted by Unitarianism, were seeking legal protection against present and future endowments being lost to, or being taken over by, any sect not in accord with the original objects of the bequests. The Society's proposal, in brief, was to create a close corporation limiting the income of its property forever to the support of one creed. In this fashion an endowment could be used to influence, if not bind, the religious thought of succeeding generations for centuries to come. To make the matter crystal clear, when the bill came before the House for passage, the representative from Blandford introduced an amendment adding a proviso "that the income of said fund shall be forever applied to the support of a learned, pious, Trinitarian Congregational minister."

An impassioned debate ensued. One group argued that the support of Christianity was essential to a republican form of government, serving to provide a moral basis for society, and that, furthermore, citizens had a legal right to dispose of their property in any manner they chose. Opponents of the Blandford petition, on the other hand, maintained that an attempt was being made to establish perpetual support for a particular creed; other denominations would be likely to seek similar protection, and the result would be sectarian strife. A majority in a parish, they held, should decide upon the disposition of endowed money, unrestricted by the dead hand of a donor.

Mann's lack of sympathy with orthodox clergymen, dating back to the traumatic experiences of his childhood with the Reverend Nathanael Emmons, automatically brought him out on the side of the liberals. When his opportunity came to speak, his principal contentions were that the legislature should not grant any irrevocable rights, impossible to amend as conditions changed; the Blandford petition would assist one group at the expense of another; and the degeneration of morals, feared by the orthodox, would occur only after the individual had "abandoned his reason as no further use and foregone his inquiries after truth." From what he had learned of European ecclesiastical history, Mann knew that men's minds would be bound by the proposed legislation, religious opinions would be made rigid and unchangeable, and religious progress would cease.

Mann's plea for religious liberty was in the tradition of Roger Williams and Thomas Jefferson. When a vote on the Blandford petition was taken, it was decisively defeated, and never again was legislation of that type presented in Massachusetts. Thereafter, acts of incorporation provided that they could be "altered or repealed at the discretion of the legislature."

Another cause for which Mann took up arms was material rather than philosophical in nature. His second speech was on behalf of the railroads, and for very practical reasons: Massachusetts was dependent upon her sister states for almost every necessity of life; the agricultural resources of the state were entirely inadequate to feed its population; the state was largely barren of mineral treasures, and wool, cotton, and silk had to be imported. The soil of Massachusetts, declared Mann, "scarcely produces anything spontaneously, and scantily requites the most devoted labor of the husbandman"—doubtless recalling the hard labor on his father's farm—adding, "We do not even grow the grain for our horses." In short, Massachusetts, which had reached a population density of eighty to the square mile, was no longer able to clothe and feed its people.

A solution to the state's dilemma, Mann was convinced, was the coming of the machine age, which he welcomed enthusiastically. "Machinery is the enlargement of human power," he said. "Here strength of mind makes up for the weakness of the body." In Massachusetts, it was necessary to look to commerce and to the manufacturing and mechanical arts for material progress. Transportation, unfortunately, lagged far behind the factory. Thus arose the need for railroads. Mann pointed out that railroads were being projected to connect the seaboard with the rapidly growing West. He argued that a railroad would advance the interests of agriculture, commerce, manufacturing, and the mechanical arts, and was essential to the continued prosperity of all branches of business—views in full accord with those of Governor Edward Everett and President John Quincy Adams.

On June 9, 1827, Josiah Quincy, then Mayor of Boston, and other citizens of Boston presented a petition to the legislature "praying for the survey of a railroad route to the Hudson." Adamant opposition to the proposal came from owners of canals and stagecoach lines. Nevertheless, by astute political maneuvering on Quincy's part and strong support from such legislators as Horace Mann, the House authorized a railroad survey to cost not more than $10,000. Two years later, the Worcester Railroad Company was chartered to run "from the coal mines in Worcester to Quinsigamond Pond and the Blackstone Canal." By the end of the 1830 session, the legislature had chartered three railroad corporations.

Minor legislation with which Mann was concerned reflected strongly held personal beliefs or biases. He served on a committee seeking ways to suppress lotteries, at every opportunity promoted temperance causes, worked for a revision of laws governing capital punishment, sponsored "a bill for mitigating, in certain cases, the penalty for the crimes of arson, burglary, and larceny," attempted to abolish imprisonment for debt laws, and in general championed the poor, the ignorant, and the unfortunate members of society.

One of Mann's major achievements as a state legislator, and for a cause close to his heart, was to improve the care of the insane and of prisoners in jails. In his own district of Dedham, shortly after Mann's election to the House, an insane inmate had died, unattended and in an unheated cell. The case was not an isolated one, for the cries and groans of the surviving inmates would "frequently disturb the neighborhood." According to a report submitted by a special House committee the previous year, 1827, other Massachusetts communities were equally backward in their treatment of the insane. The committee found six classes of inmates in the state's jails. The first five were various types of criminals and debtors. The sixth group was described as "lunatics and persons furiously mad." Concerning the last, the committee insisted that "something must be done. . . .The situation of these poor wretched beings calls for some redress. . . .They seem to have been considered as out of the protection of the laws." Even when the jailers were humane individuals, they had no qualifications or professional training for caring for the insane. As Jonathan Messerli notes, "less attention was given to the cleanliness and comfort of lunatics than to farm animals at a county fair. Some of the inmates had literally wallowed in their own filth for more than twenty years."[6]

As early as 1818, the McLean Asylum, a division of the Massachusetts General Hospital, had opened its doors. It was, however, a private institution catering largely to individuals and families who could afford the high cost of extended hospitalization. It did not meet the needs of lower and middle-class patients.

In the same year as the legislative committee's report, the public was profoundly shocked to read the facts discovered by a voluntary organization, the Prison Discipline Society. For example, in one prison, the Society's account read, five lunatics were confined in cells "which were almost dark dungeons. It was difficult, after the door was open, to see them distinctly. The ventilation was so incomplete, that more than one person entering them has found the air so fetid, as to produce nauseousness, and almost vomiting. The old straw on which they were laid, and their filthy garments were such as to make their insanity more hopeless." One inmate, confined in unheated quarters, had been out of his cell only twice in eight years. Frequently, there was no heat in the prisons even in the coldest weather.

In 1828, following the two reports, Horace Mann made a stirring appeal for action, stating as a principle that "the insane are the wards of the state." It was obvious that the towns and counties were incapable of providing proper care for these unfortunate creatures. A bill for the "Safe keeping of lunatics and persons furiously mad" previously had been filed in the legislature and Mann now moved that it be referred to a committee of which he was chairman. The committee's first step was to inquire into prevailing provisions for the insane throughout the state. Its findings confirmed the earlier investigations, revealing the existence of an intolerable state of affairs. A survey of eighty-nine

towns discovered there were "two hundred and eighty-nine lunatics, or persons furiously mad, that one hundred and sixty-one of
that number are now in confinement in the following places, viz:
in poor houses and houses of industry, seventy-eight; in private
houses, thirty-seven; in jails and houses of correction, nineteen;
in insane hospitals, ten; place of confinement not specifically
stated, seventeen." The report was necessarily incomplete, for
many communities had failed to respond to the committee's
inquiry.

The mentally ill in Massachusetts, according to the Mann
committee report, had been confined for periods ranging up to
forty-five years though guilty of no crimes. They were without
therapeutic treatment. The situation could only be corrected,
Mann stated to the legislature, through the erection of a state
hospital, which it was estimated would cost $30,000 for a building
large enough to accommodate 130 patients. The committee declined to estimate the annual maintenance expense, but expressed its belief "that proper medical treatment, kind and careful
attention to the comforts, and the malady of the insane, can be
furnished at an expense not exceeding the ability of the great
mass of our citizens to defray."

The legislature, doubtless sensitive to the cumulative impact of
the several critical and widely publicized reports which had been
issued, acted with unusual promptness in adopting a resolution
offered by Horace Mann "for erecting a lunatic hospital." A site
was selected at Worcester and a legislative commission, of course
including Mann as chairman, was appointed to oversee the building and organization of the projected hospital. The location was
to be on a twelve-acre plot, "of a singularly regular and beautiful
elevation commanding a view of the town, and the rich scenery of
the surrounding country, sufficiently near to the market, and
principal places of business, for necessary accommodation, and
yet so retired as to be secure from improper intrusion or distur-
bance and within a short distance of the head waters of the
Blackstone Canal."

A report of the commissioners, prepared in 1832 by Mann,
expressed optimism regarding the curability of mental disease.
"Until a period comparatively recent," it stated, "insanity has
been deemed as an incurable disease. The universal opinion has

been that it was an awful visitation from Heaven, and that no human agency could reverse the judgement by which it was inflicted. During the prevalence of this inauspicious belief, as all efforts to restore the insane would be deemed unavailing, they of course would be unattempted." The report concluded on a hopeful note: "It is now abundantly demonstrated that with appropriate medical and moral treatment insanity yields with more readiness than ordinary diseases."

In 1833, the new institution, the first of its kind in the United States, was completed, meticulously guided by Horace Mann and other members of the board of trustees appointed by Governor Levi Lincoln. The patients admitted at the beginning were brought almost entirely from jails and other correctional institutions of the state. Under the leadership of Dr. Samuel B. Woodward (later the first president of the Association of Medical Superintendents of American Institutions for the Insane, which became the American Psychiatric Association), the Worcester hospital gained a national reputation and served as a model for other states, especially as a result of its success in therapeutic treatments. Within the first year, the number of applicants exceeded the hospital's physical facilities. An additional appropriation of $25,000 was approved by the legislature in 1835 for enlarging the building. But the number of mentally ill persons seemed to increase faster than the general population, and within a few years the Worcester hospital was suffering from ills common to such institutions down to the present day: overcrowding, declining curability rates, and an influx of lower-class groups. Nevertheless, in the auspicious opening days, Horace Mann saw hopeful omens for the future. A letter to his sister Lydia, three months after the hospital's formal opening, expresses his feelings:

I hear from Worcester very frequently, and the accounts are most flattering. Everything seems to have commenced under very favorable auspices, and so far the success has very far transcended my most sanguime expectations. Individuals who had for years while subjected to the severe rigors of confinement in jails and Houses of Correction, been so frantic and ferocious, that their keepers had not ventured to go into their cells, had not been at Worcester a week before the powerful and reviving influences of good air and suitable diet and cleanliness and warmth with the expression of kindness on the part of their attendants, had so far transformed them into men, that they became quiet and manageable, and declared themselves happy in their new condition.[7]

The last of Horace Mann's notable accomplishments as a state legislator—one which was destined to affect him personally far more than the pioneer institution in Worcester—was an epoch-making education bill, "An Act Relating to Common Schools," which became a law on April 20, 1837. At the beginning of the year, Mann had been elected president of the Senate on the first ballot, a tribute to his high standing among his colleagues in that body. Previously, he had paid slight attention to educational problems, refusing, for example, an appointment to the Committee on Education in order to serve on the more influential Judiciary Committee.

Some of Mann's closest friends had helped to organize the American Institute of Instruction to work for common school reform. During the 1836-37 legislative session, the Institute submitted a memorial to the legislature recommending the appointment of a Superintendent of the Common Schools of the Commonwealth, while Governor Everett, in his opening address, proposed the creation of a State Board of Education. The governor saw education as "the solid basis of equality, the most effectual means of redressing the hardships of fortune." The people were required by law, he pointed out, to support education because it had always laid "the cornerstone of the social edifice on the intelligence of the people." Recognizing the great social contribution of the schools, he stressed the importance of more commodious buildings, a lengthened school term, scientific apparatus, libraries, and, above all, well-qualified teachers.

A windfall of $2,000,000 from the federal government came to the state of Massachusetts in payment for the services of its militia in the War of 1812. Horace Mann and a few other enlightened members of the legislature urged that the money should be used to improve public education throughout the state. As Mann phrased the matter, the fund could be invested in "some great, permanent, public object, where its benefits will be universal, enduring and progressive," or, conversely, it would be frittered away for "objects of a transient nature that at the end of a year neither the money nor the object will remain." The political-minded legislators, convinced that their constituents were mainly interested in lower taxes, voted, however, to allot only half the money to the school fund and distributed the remainder to the towns for roads, bridges, almshouses, jails, and "other public objects of expenditure." Clearly, public schools were not yet regarded as a profitable issue politically; parents still placed tax savings ahead of better education for their children. Horace Mann saw it as his duty to change that benighted attitude.

Critics have questioned why Massachusetts did not follow the recommendation of the American Institute of Education by appointing a top state official, with supervisory authority over the schools, as became the custom among other states. Doubtless, there was a fear of centralization in the Commonwealth, where decentralized control had been carried to extremes. In any event, Governor Everett regarded a state board of education as a first step in bringing some order and system into the common schools of Massachusetts.

Even a state board sans executive power was not established without a struggle. James G. Carter, chairman of the House Committee on Education, reported a bill to the floor of the House, where it met strong opposition and was defeated two to one. A move for reconsideration met the same fate. Carter, a staunch, long-time fighter for public education, persisted, and when the Senate passed the bill, brought the measure up for a third time. Enough representatives were persuaded to change their votes to carry the measure, and Governor Everett signed it into law. Horace Mann had helped to shepherd the bill through the upper house and signed it as president of the Senate.

As created, the Board of Education consisted of ten members: the governor and lieutenant governor, serving ex-officio, and eight appointed members serving eight-year terms, in staggered order. The Board, under the law, was primarily an information agency, without real powers. It was charged with preparing a printed abstract of the school returns, mainly statistics, for presentation to the legislature before each session; it could appoint its own Secretary and fix his compensation; and, under the direction of the Board, it was the Secretary's duty "to collect information of the actual condition and efficiency of the common schools and other means of popular education; and to diffuse as widely as possible, throughout every part of the Commonwealth, information of the most approved and successful methods of arranging the studies and conducting the education of the young." Whether the Board would function in a perfunctory, futile fashion or would accomplish much through persuasion and education depended principally on finding an effective Secretary.

The personnel of the new Board was selected with the greatest of care by Governor Everett, who aimed to appoint men whose names would carry prestige and be widely representative. The final list included Jared Sparks, historian, president of Harvard, and a Unitarian; Edmund Dwight, manufacturer, philanthropist, and Whig; Emerson Davis, Congregational minister; Edward A. Newton, banker and leading Episcopalian; Thomas Robbins, another leader in Congregational circles; Robert Rantoul, Jr., Democratic politician and Unitarian; James G. Carter, Whig representative from Lancaster; and Horace Mann.

The educators of the state expected that James G. Carter would be selected as Secretary of the Board. Carter's labors as a teacher and writer on public education had been indefatigable. There was surprise and some disappointment, therefore, when, instead, the Board turned to Horace Mann. The reasons, it appears, were that the Board was seeking a person who had qualities beyond those of a professional educator: prominence in public life, political power, a dedicated and unselfish personality, great nervous and physical energy, and the ability to convert the people to a belief in public education. This paragon, the Board decided, it had found in Mann.

To convince Mann that he should accept the position after the Board came to its decision was a more difficult matter. He had not anticipated that he would be considered for the appointment. On the other hand, he fully recognized its potential significance, writing that it was "a most responsible and important office, bearing more effectually, if well executed, upon the coming welfare of the State than any other office in it." But, he asked himself, according to his diary, "Ought I to think of filling this high and responsible office? Can I adequately perform its duties? Will my greater zeal in the cause than that of others supply the deficiency in point of talent and information?"[8]

Other doubts also rose in Mann's mind. He had become a

prominent attorney with an income of three thousand dollars a year. As president of the Senate, he was one of the state's leading citizens. The financial sacrifice would be considerable; the Secretary's salary was set by the Board at one thousand dollars, to which Edmund Dwight added five hundred. No office, clerical assistance, postage and stationery, or travel funds were provided. Further, as Mann foresaw, writing in his journal, "Whoever shall undertake that task must encounter privation, labor, and infinite annoyance from an infinite number of schemers."

Finally, after lengthy meditation, casting aside all doubts and fears, on June 30, 1837, Mann tendered his resignation as a member of the Board of Education and accepted the Secretary-ship. Again he turned to his journal to record his inner thoughts on that momentous day:

Henceforth so long as I hold this office I devote myself to the supremest welfare of mankind upon earth. An inconceivably greater labor is under-taken. With the highest degree of prosperity, results will manifest them-selves but slowly. The harvest is far from the seed-time. *Faith* is the only sustainer. I have faith in the improvability of the human race,—in their accelerating improvability.[9]

Thus did Horace Mann enter upon a twelve-year span destined to shape his own future and to influence the lives of generations of children to come.

CHAPTER 3

Massachusetts Schools—Pre-Mann

When Horace Mann accepted the Secretaryship of the Massachusetts Board of Education in 1837, the condition of the state's public schools would have appalled the most stouthearted. In his *Second* and *Twelfth Annual Reports,* Mann takes a retrospective look at the system for which he had now assumed responsibility:

Facts incontrovertibly show, that for a series of years previous to 1837, the school system of Massachusetts had been running down. Schoolhouses had been growing old, while new ones were rarely erected. School districts were divided, so that each part was obliged to support its schools on the moiety of a fund, the whole of which was a scanty allowance.[10]

A complexity of other problems afflicted the schools. Among them, as described by Mann, was child labor "in factories, in the shoe-making business, and in other mechanical employments," which "swelled the already enormous amount of non-attendance and irregularity." There was no standardization of textbooks, as a consequence of which "the multiplicity of different books in the same school embarrassed all kinds of instruction." The general level of teaching was extremely low, for "the business of school-keeping fell more and more into the hands of youth and inexperience; so that, in rare instances only, did the maturity of years preside over the indiscretions of the young." A constant turnover of teachers occurred, subjecting the children to the "perpetual renewals and unskillfulness of first experiments." Since the dissolution of territorial parishes, in 1833, clergymen no longer superintended the schools as part of their parochial duty. Most destructive of all, doubtless, was the fact that "the private school system was rapidly absorbing the funds, patronizing the talent, and withdrawing the sympathy, which belonged to the Public Schools."

Mann could only conclude from his overall review of the situation "that the Common School system of Massachusetts had fallen into a state of general unsoundness and debility,"[11] the schools lacked supervision, and many of the most intelligent and wealthy citizens had lost interest in their welfare.

It had not always been thus in Massachusetts and New England. Horace Mann may have exaggerated in his *Tenth Annual Report,* commenting on the Pilgrims and education, when he stated: "The Pilgrim Fathers who colonized Massachusetts Bay made a bolder innovation upon all pre-existing policy and usages than the world had ever known since the commencement of the Christian era. They adopted special and costly means to train up the whole body of the people to industry, to intelligence, to virtue, and to independent thought." Mann notes that as early as 1635 the public-record book of Boston lists the employment of two schoolmasters. In the same year, Boston's celebrated Latin School was established. A year later, the General Court founded Harvard College. The records are conclusive that the New England Puritans considered education and religion inseparable. The proportion of Cambridge and Oxford graduates among their leaders was amazingly high.

The most radical step to promote the cause of education was taken by the General Court on June 14, 1642, when it enacted a compulsory education law. Municipal authorities were enjoined to see that every child within their respective jurisdictions should be educated. Parents were required to furnish town selectmen data for a census and were subject to fines for refusing to provide the information or for neglecting to send their children to school. The act stipulated further that religious instruction should be given to all children; they must be taught "perfectly to read the English tongue" and be knowledgeable about the capital laws. To provide training in education and employment useful to the Commonwealth, matters neglected by many parents and masters, the act continued, all parents and masters must "breed and bring up their children and apprentices in some honest, lawful calling, labor, or employment, either in husbandry or some other trade profitable for themselves and the Commonwealth, if they will not or can not train them up in learning to fit them for higher employments."[12]

Here, Horace Mann remarks, "were recognized and embodied in a public statute the highest principles of political economy and of social well-being, the universal education of children, and the prevention of drones or non-producers among men." Under the law, parents and masters who failed, after being admonished, to perform their duty could lose custody of their children.

The 1642 law enjoined compulsory education. Unfortunately, however, it did not make education free, nor did it impose any penalty upon a municipal government for neglecting to maintain a school or to provide teachers. Consequently, the law was unenforceable. Instruction still had to be carried on at home, in voluntary schools, or by private teachers. Another law, enacted on November 11, 1647, endeavored to remedy the deficiency by making the support of schools compulsory, and education both universal and free. This statute, the first general school law recorded in American history, required every town with fifty householders to appoint a teacher "to teach all such children as shall resort to him to write and to read," and every town with one hundred families or householders to "set up a grammar school," whose master should be "able to instruct youth so far as they may be fitted for the university." Familiarly referred to as the "old deluder" act, its philosophical basis is expressed in a preamble:

It being one chief object of that old deluder, Satan, to keep men from the knowledge of the Scriptures, as in former times by keeping them in an unknown tongue, so in these latter times by persuading from the use of tongues, that so at least the true sense and meaning of the original might be clouded by false glosses of saint-seeming deceivers, that learning may not be buried in the grave of our fathers in the church and commonwealth, the Lord assisting our endeavours, . . .[13]

The act then went on to specify requirements for the appointment of teachers and the establishment of schools. The chief responsibility for education remained, however, in the hands of the parents and the masters of schools. Towns could still decide whether or not to levy taxes to maintain schools. School attendance was not compulsory and there was no provision for forcing parents or children to use the facilities provided. If citizens preferred, they could have their children educated at home or in private schools. Nor were free schools mandatory; under the law they might be supported by the parents of the pupils who attended or by the towns, if a majority so voted. The trend, however, was toward public support, and as Governor John Winthrop wrote, "Divers free schools were erected, as at Roxbury and at Boston." The cost of the schools outgrew the ability of parents and guardians to support them. By the middle of the eighteenth century, education was practically free.

For a century or more after the establishment of the Massachusetts Bay colony, schools were all associated with towns, but then the population began to move out of the settled communities and scatter into the wilderness. A single school or a single church no longer met the needs of the people. As a consequence, a curious new development began, "traveling schools" or "moving schools," which continued in existence until Horace Mann's time. Instead of the children going to the school, the school came to the children. For a certain length of time, the school was set up in one corner of the district, then moved on to another until the circuit had been completed. Even grammar schools circulated. The system naturally tended to diffuse education, making depth and thoroughness impossible, and disrupting any centralized control. Sections which had been served by the moving schools soon began to demand permanent schools of their own, and the former central school gradually was replaced by district schools. The system of local educational autonomy which evolved was a serious impediment to educational progress, as Horace Mann soon discovered. Hinsdale notes that the introduction of the local district system was marked by "contentions, school politics, irresponsibility, favoritism, small ideas, and wastefulness; small schools, short terms, low ideals, lack of oversight, poor teachers, and poor teaching"[14]—all problems which confronted Mann when he assumed the Secretaryship of the Board of Education.

Following the Revolution, the Massachusetts legislature, in 1789, passed an act which Horace Mann damned as "the most unfortunate law on the subject of Common Schools ever enacted in the State." The law formally authorized towns to divide themselves into districts. As a result, there occurred an unbalanced school development in the Commonwealth. Some districts, usually the wealthier ones, made adequate provision for their schools. Other districts did little or nothing. Subsequent legislation further weakened the schools, until by 1827, in E.I.F. Williams's words, "the people became apathetic to the schools, schools became poorer, and the people became still more listless and apathetic. The common schools had become cheap. They had poor support, poor teachers, poor pupils, poor buildings, poor textbooks, poor or nonexistent equipment—and poor *popular* support."

During the second half of the eighteenth century private academies began to be founded, in part because of the decline of the public schools. Inevitably, they led to the latter's further deterioration. At first, the private schools were supported from nonpublic funds, but then the legislature adopted a policy of grants of public land to them. The academies were far better equipped to prepare boys for college than were the decaying grammar schools, since they offered a considerable range of classes in the liberal arts and sciences. In proportion as the academies and other private schools proliferated, however, the common schools degenerated. Parents who were able to pay for their children's education sent them to the academies and private schools, while those lacking financial means patronized the public schools. Class distinctions, a new phenomenon in Massachusetts, arose. The best teachers and the best pupils turned to the private schools. The most intelligent and the wealthier members of the community sent their children to the academies, concurrently losing interest in and resisting adequate tax support for public schools. In the popular mind the common schools came to denote "pauper schools," attended by children of the poorer classes only.

Educational conditions in other states were at least equally deplorable. In 1834 there were no less than 100,000 illiterate voters in the state of Pennsylvania and 25,000 children there did not attend school. In Virginia, a fourth of the persons applying for marriage licenses could not write. In Ohio, nearly one-half of the districts were without schoolhouses. Of 1,840,000 children of school age in 1832, excluding New York, 1,400,000 lacked common instruction.

But voices crying in the wilderness were beginning to be heard. Influential writers on education were publishing articles and pamphlets urging better preparation for teachers. In Concord, Vermont, Samuel R. Hall established a normal school for teachers. One of the most effective and persistent spokesmen for educational reform was James G. Carter, chairman of the Massachusetts House Committee on Education and eloquent advocate of normal schools and public education. Writing in 1824, Carter deplored the decline in the quality of the public schools, warning that, "If the policy of the legislature in regard to free schools for the last twenty years be not changed, the institution which has been the glory of New England will, in twenty years more, be extinct." Another powerful and active leader was Henry Barnard, who in the eighteen-thirties began the improvement of the public school systems of Connecticut and Rhode Island and subsequently became the first United States Commissioner of Education. Also influential were a number of teachers' organizations which began to be formed, particularly the American Institute of Education, which held its first meeting in Boston in 1830. In his *Tenth Annual Report*, Horace Mann paid high tribute to the Institute's contributions:

The Institute may justly be considered the source of all the improvements in education which have since been made in New England and the other Northern States; and its influence is slowly diffusing itself through the uncongenial regions of the South.[15]

Despite these propitious omens, the outlook for the public schools when Mann became Secretary of the Board of Education was grim. As summarized by an educational historian, William R. Odell, the sad facts were:

1. State law had encouraged decentralization to a disastrous degree.
2. Public interest in education was declining.
3. Financial support for education was decreasing.
4. Public or free schools were held in contempt by upper classes who sent their children increasingly to private schools.
5. The net result was short terms, dilapidated and unsanitary schools, untrained and underpaid teachers, and irrational methods of teaching.[16]

CHAPTER 4

Teachers and Teaching

In the first of his twelve *Annual Reports,* Horace Mann stressed emphatically the need for competent teachers. "Teaching," he states, "is the most difficult of all arts, and the profoundest of all sciences." Elaborating on the importance of teaching, Mann adds:

In its absolute perfection, it would involve a complete knowledge of the whole being to be taught, and of the precise manner in which every possible application would affect it; that is, a complete knowledge of all the powers and capacities of the individual, with their exact proportions and relations to each other, and a knowledge, how, at any hour or moment, to select and apply, from a universe of means, the one then exactly apposite to its ever-changing condition.[17]

Teaching also involves, according to Mann, "a knowledge of the principal laws of physical, mental and moral growth." Such basic subjects as arithmetic and grammar, in his view, comprise but a small part of the teachings in a school. "The sentiments and passions get more lessons than the intellect." A true paragon would be required to meet the injunctions laid upon teachers by the Massachusetts law, cited by Mann. Teachers were directed to impress upon their pupils "the principles of piety, justice and a sacred regard to truth, love to their country, humanity and universal benevolence, sobriety, industry and frugality, chastity, moderation and temperance, and those other virtues, which are the ornament of human society."[18] Mann seriously questioned whether under the existing system, or lack of system, of investigating the qualifications of teachers and making appointments, it was realistic or reasonable to expect that "the elevated purposes contemplated by the law" were being or could be met.

During his first year as Secretary of the Board of Education, Mann discussed with educational leaders and "intelligent men" the "extensive want of competent teachers for the common schools." He concludes that "the teachers are as good as public opinion has demanded." School committees defended their appointment of incompetent persons by pointing out "the utter impossibility of obtaining better for the compensation offered." Even in the larger communities—Boston, Salem, Lowell, etc.—where salaries were relatively generous, wages were low. For the state as a whole, the average salary per month, inclusive of board, paid to male teachers was $25.44, and to female teachers, $11.38. Exclusive of board, the average annual salary was $185.28 for male teachers and $64.56 for women teachers.

While recognizing the school committees' difficulty in finding devoted and accomplished teachers for the schools, Mann maintained that it was within "their power, and is a most responsible and solemn part of their duty, not to inflict upon the children of a whole district the calamity of an ignorant, ill-tempered or profane teacher."[19] The school law required local committees to obtain evidence of the good moral character of all teachers and to learn "by personal examination their literary qualifications and capacity for the government of schools." Because such an examination was time-consuming, however, Mann discovered that in a majority of instances it was "either wholly omitted or is formal and superficial, rather than intent and thorough."

Several years later, Mann noted considerable improvement in the situation. In his *Fifth Annual Report* he found, "In many towns there has been a most earnest and importunate demand for those of satisfactory attainments and unexceptionable character."[20] Candidates were being given thorough examinations, both in regard to their literary qualifications and to their ability to manage a school. School committees were taking a more active role in providing counsel and aid to the teachers. Teachers themselves were beginning to organize to exchange views and to discuss relevant subjects; a number of such assemblies were addressed by Horace Mann, at the invitation of the teachers themselves. On the other hand, the demand for higher qualifications outstripped the supply. There was simply an insufficient number of well-educated, experienced teachers to man all the schools where they were needed.

Mann's *Fourth Annual Report* analyzes in detail "a few of the qualifications essential to those who undertake the momentous task of training the children of the State."[21] At the top, he places *a knowledge of common-school subjects.* In his judgment, "Teachers should have a perfect knowledge of the rudimental branches which are required by law to be taught in our schools," adding that "teachers should be able to teach *subjects,* not manuals merely." Furthermore, this knowledge should be thorough and critical, "familiar like the alphabet," enabling the teacher to carry on instruction and listen to recitations while maintaining discipline and keeping the school under proper control without having to devote his entire attention to the class in progress. Up-to-date facts are also essential in geography, for example, which cannot be taught correctly without an awareness of changes going on more or less constantly around the world. A broad, superficial knowledge of many subjects, Mann held, "is no equivalent for a mastership in the rudiments," asserting in the *Fourth Annual Report* that:

The leading, prevailing defect in the intellectual department of our schools, is a want of thoroughness,—a proneness to be satisfied with a verbal memory of rules, instead of a comprehension of principles,—with a knowledge of the names of things, instead of a knowledge of the things themselves;—or, if some knowledge of the thing is gained, it is too apt to be a knowledge of them as isolated facts, and unaccompanied by a knowledge of the relations, which subsist between them, and bind them into a scientific whole.

The next principal qualification in a teacher, after thoroughness of subject knowledge, is listed by Mann as *the art of teaching.* "The ability to acquire, and the ability to impart," he points out, "are wholly different talents," a fact recognized, for example, in Francis Bacon's remark that "the art of well-delivering the knowledge we possess is among the secrets, left to be discovered by future generations." Thus, school committees not infrequently find that teachers who have passed an examination acceptably fail in the schoolroom, because they lack facility in communicating what they know. Aptness to teach, in Mann's opinion, "includes the presentation of the different parts of a subject, in a natural order." It also "embraces a knowledge of methods and processes," which are "indefinitely various." The aim should be to accomplish the object in "an easy and natural manner." The person thoroughly proficient in the art of teaching "is acquainted, not only with common methods for common minds, but with peculiar methods for pupils of peculiar dispositions and temperaments; and he is acquainted with the principles of all methods, whereby he can vary his plan, according to any difference of circumstances." There should be no "one, inflexible, immutable course of instruction," forcing everyone into a common mold.

Point three in Mann's catalog of requirements for a successful teacher was *management, government, and discipline of a school.* A person may possess literary competence and ability to teach, but still lack the power to manage and govern a school. There is no necessary connection, Mann observes, between these various qualities. Under the heading of management, he lists various factors: the organization of classes, to recognize slow and fast learners; discretion in assignment of lessons to avoid leaving certain pupils with idle time on their hands and others so overloaded that they cannot do their work thoroughly; the preservation of order, to prevent confusion on one hand and military formality on the other; and the necessity of system in all the school's operations.

Even more difficult is the government and discipline of a school, "because the consequences of error are still more disastrous." With a strong aversion to corporal punishment, Mann viewed the chastisement of pupils as "the last resort, the ultimate resource, acknowledged, on all hands, to be a relic of barbarism, and yet authorized, because the community, although they feel it to be a great evil, have not yet devised and applied an antidote." From one point of view, the teacher has an unfair advantage, for he or she is lawmaker, lawyer, jury, judge, and executive officer, as well as plaintiff. "Every child ought to find, at school, the affection and the wisdom, which he has left at home," Mann comments, "or, if he has left neither wisdom nor affection at home, there is so much more need, that he should find them at school." A school should be governed at all times with a steady hand, "for it is injurious to the children to alternate between the extremes of an easy and a sharp discipline."

The school law directed teachers to inculcate *good behavior* in all youth placed in their charge. A direct connection exists, claims Mann, between good manners and good morals. The effects of civility or discourtesy are felt directly by society. It is highly important, therefore, that "a right direction should be given to the growing mind" in the schoolroom and the playground. Since the behavior of the teacher is likely to be emulated by the pupils, the teacher should pay strict regard "to deportment, dress, conversation, and all personal habits, that constitute the difference between a gentleman and a clown." Eccentric behavior may be tolerated in others, but not in one from whom "fifty or a hundred children are to form their manners."

The fifth and last qualification for good teachers discussed by Mann is *morals*. Moral character, he states emphatically, is an "indispensable, all-controlling requisite" in the selection and appointment of teachers. No considerations of friendship, relationship to members of school committees, "or any selfish or personal motive whatever" should be permitted to influence the choice of teachers. Chief responsibility in this matter in Massachusetts rested with school committees, whose duty it was to insure that no one "who is profane, or intemperate, or addicted to low associations, or branded with the stigma of any vice, may be installed over the pure minds of the young, as their guide and exemplar."

To illustrate the influence and worth of a great teacher, Mann cites an anecdote about Nathaniel Bowditch, who when he sailed on an East Indian voyage "took pains to instruct the crew of the ship, in the art of navigation. Every sailor on board, during that voyage, became afterwards a captain of a ship. Such are the natural consequences of associating with a man, whose mind is intent upon useful knowledge and whose actions are born of benevolence."[22]

The part played by the child in the learning process is stressed by Mann, who concludes that "though much may be done by others to aid, yet the effective labor must be performed by the learner himself." He comments further:

Knowledge cannot be poured into a child's mind, like fluid from one

vessel to another. The pupil may do something by intuition, but generally there must be a conscious effort on his part. He is not a passive
recipient, but an active, voluntary agent. He must do more than admit or
welcome; he must reach out, and grasp, and bring home. It is the duty of
the teacher to bring knowledge within arm's length of the learner; and he
must break down its masses into portions so minute, that they can be
taken up and appropriated, one by one; but the final appropriating act
must be the learner's. . . . Hence all effective teaching must have reference to this indispensable, consummating act and effort of the learner.[23]

The first requisite of sound teaching, then, according to Mann,
is to awaken in the child's mind the desire to learn. For instance, if
he is bored, as he probably is, in long periods spent in learning the
alphabet, he resists learning. "Until a desire to learn exists within
the child," Mann remarks, "some foreign force must constantly
be supplied to keep him agoing; but from the moment that a
desire is excited, he is self-motive, and goes alone."

How to make the teaching profession more attractive to able
young men is a central theme of Mann's *Eleventh Annual Report.*
The choice of a career, he points out, is chiefly influenced by two
factors: "The first of these is the natural tendency of the
mind,—its predisposition towards one pursuit rather than towards another"; and, second, the human desire for pleasure, for
wealth, for honor, or other rewards. "The qualities which predis-
pose their possessor to become the companion, guide, and
teacher of children," Mann lists as "good sense, lively religious
sensibilities, practical, unaffected benevolence, a genuine sympathy with the young, and that sunny, genial temperament which
always sees its own cheerfulness reflected from the ever-open
mirror of a child's face."[24]

Many persons are born with these requisite qualities, Mann
believed, but unfortunately when they arrive at the proper age to
decide upon their life's work, they discover that the noble profession of teaching "is neither honored by distinction nor rewarded
by emolument." If they make inquiries, "they cannot find a single
public-school teacher who has acquired wealth by the longest and
most devoted life of labor. They cannot find one who has been
promoted to the presidency of a college, or to a professorship in
it; nor one who has been elected or appointed to fill any distinguished civil station." For such reasons, they are repelled by the

teaching profession, and if they become teachers at all, "it is only for a brief period, and for some collateral purpose; and when their temporary end is gained, they sink it still lower by their avowed or well-understood reasons for abandoning it."[25] According to Mann, there had been hundreds or even thousands of such cases.

The root of the problem appeared to be the extremely low wages for teachers prevailing throughout the Union. In Maine, Mann cited figures to show that the average salary of men teachers was $15.40 and of women teachers $4.80 per month. The corresponding figures for New Hampshire were $13.50 and $5.65; in Vermont, $12.00 and $4.75; in Connecticut, $16.00 and $6.50; in New York, $14.96 and $6.69; in Pennsylvania, $17.02 and $10.09; in Ohio, $15.42 and $8.73; in Indiana, $12.00 and $6.00; and in Michigan, $12.71 and $5.36. When "compared with what is paid to cashiers of banks, to secretaries of insurance-companies, to engineers upon railroads, to superintendents in factories, to custom-house officers, Navy agents, and so forth," Mann commented, "it will then be seen what pecuniary temptations there are on every side, drawing enterprising and talented young men from the ranks of the teacher's profession."[26]

Nor do teachers fare any better in terms of social standing. Mann notes that they are effectively barred from political honors, they cannot engage in trade or commercial activities, and in fact are "shut out from all the paths that lead to fortune or to fame." Thus "aspiring and highly-endowed youth" find few attractions in teaching; those ambitious for wealth go into trade; the mechanically inclined apply themselves to the useful arts; the politically ambitious connect themselves with parties; medicine and the ministry draw those with certain other talents and tastes.

Among the remedies for this deplorable state of affairs proposed by Mann were higher qualifications for those admitted to the teaching profession; a material lengthening of the school year, perhaps to ten months; and salaries commensurate with those the same persons could command in other fields. Professional training, a school term long enough to provide almost continuous employment, and adequate compensation, Mann felt, would overcome the most serious disadvantages under which teachers were then working.

Mann expressed indignation at the disproportion between the wages of male and female teachers, which seemed to him "indefensible on any principle of justice or policy." His *Sixth Annual Report* notes a ratio of more than two and a half to one in the state of Massachusetts. "But why," he asks, "should a woman receive less than two-fifths as much as a man, for services which in no respect are of inferior value?" The practice's "inevitable consequence is to degrade the standard of female qualifications for teaching, and this is followed as inevitably by a deterioration in the quality of the instruction given." Because of low wages and the willingness to settle for teachers of limited attainments for small children, very young girls were selected as teachers by school committees. "This," remarks Mann, "adds inexperience in government to deficiency in knowledge and immaturity in character." If the compensation of female teachers were suitably increased, they could "afford to expend more money and time in qualifying themselves for the better discharge of their responsible duties." At the time Mann was writing, he observed that women teachers were receiving "less than is paid to the better class of female operatives in factories."[27]

Mann was firmly convinced that women teachers were superior to men in many respects: "All those differences of organization and temperament which individualize the sexes point to the female as the guide and guardian of young children." By nature, Mann saw her as having "a preponderance of affection over intellect," and therefore possessing a disposition more in harmony with young children of both sexes. Children "aspire after the sympathy of a nature kindred to their own. . . .They need kindness and not force." Mann was pleased therefore to record the fact that women were being employed as public school teachers much more extensively than in the past. But this did not exempt them, in Mann's view, from "a duty imperative upon them so to improve their minds, by study, by reading, by reflection, and by attending courses of instruction on the subject of teaching."

The methodology of teaching was of great interest to Mann and he dwells upon the subject from time to time throughout the *Annual Reports* and in his other writings. His fame rests chiefly on his achievements as an educational administrator and leader, rather than as an educational theorist, but his contributions to improved teaching practices are far from insignificant, both as to general methods and the teaching of special subjects.

Concerning the purpose of education, Mann viewed education as a broad functional process, bringing about a harmonious relation of body, intellect, and spirit. He favored, accordingly, an education that would develop the individual in as many functional ways as possible. Health education was needed for physical development. Ethical training was required to produce persons who would love truth and rise "above deciding great and eternal principles upon narrow and selfish grounds." Education must "take the accumulations in knowledge, of almost six thousand years and transfer the vast treasure to posterity," but "preserve the good and repudiate the evil." On the practical side, "education must prepare our citizens to become municipal officers, intelligent jurors, honest witnesses, legislators, or competent judges of legislation,—in fine, to fill all the manifold relations of life." Finally, "education, alone, can conduct us to that enjoyment which is, at once, best in quality and infinite in quantity."

Various passages in the *Reports* examine questions of mental growth and the development of thinking. Mann strongly supports the inductive as opposed to the dogmatic method of instruction. As he defines the term, the latter "consists in laying down abstract rules, formulas, or theorems, in a positive, authoritative manner, and requiring the forms of words in which the abstractions are committed to memory." The principle currently being taught is received by the learner with or without understanding and without questioning its truth or falsity. The inductive method, on the other hand, "exhibits, explains, illustrates, exemplifies, and educes, and then submits the whole to the learner's intelligence, to be received or discarded."

It is important, Mann wrote, for the teacher to recognize individual differences among students. An article in the *Common School Journal* in 1843 emphasizes the point: "the difference between men in regard to their bodily vigor, fleetness, dexterity, is great, but is as nothing compared with the differences in their intellectual strength and sagacity,—in their celerity and grasp of thought."[28]

The matter of motivation in learning also received much attention from Mann. Among the means recommended were the presentation of the subject matter in a simple, natural order; sincere effort by the teacher to win the confidence and love of the pupils; encouragement of extensive reading on the part of the children; and thorough mastery of their subjects by teachers. To be avoided were the motive of fear, which "will destroy interest, and will speedily create disgust"; rote learning, such as the "stupendous folly" of teaching children to read without understanding what they read; and the practice of emulation or the stimulation of excessive rivalry among pupils.

Mann wrote much, too, about the conduct of the recitation, considered an important part of the teaching procedure. "The hour of recitation" he saw as "the hour of reckoning; the place of recitation is the place for weighing and gauging the amount of recognition made by the pupils." At the same time, he warned, "I fear that too much value is ordinarily attached to the recitation. I fear it is often regarded as an object, and not as an instrument; as the goal, and not as the path that leads to it." Reverting to an earlier point, it was observed that too often children recite merely on the words of the lesson rather than on the meaning of it. Other pitfalls were noted, as, for example:

The teacher can insure any number of imperfect recitations by giving too long or too difficult lessons,—lessons beyond the ability of the scholars to learn; and thus a mere mistake in judgement, on the part of the teacher, may lead to discouragement or fraud on the part of the pupils.

Failures in recitations were also caused, according to Mann, by the use of poor or improper questions, by not questioning the pupils in random order, and by neglecting to review sufficiently. It was clearly recognized by Mann that the function of the recitation was to guide, stimulate, and integrate learning, and not merely to hear lessons.

Of all the subjects in the common school curriculum, Mann paid most attention to reading and spelling. A large portion of the *Second Annual Report* is devoted to proposed changes in the teaching of reading. The first step urged by Mann was abandonment of the standard American practice of beginning by memorizing the alphabet and then learning to read two- and three-letter combinations, and instead to begin reading by teaching entire words. The old system was a complete failure, he asserted, resulting in a situation where "more than eleven-twelfths of all the children in the reading classes, in our schools, do not understand the meaning of the words they read; they do not master the sense of the reading lessons, and the ideas and feelings intended by the author to be conveyed to, and excited in, the reader's mind, still rest in the author's intention, never having yet reached the place of their destination."

Historians of education have concluded that Horace Mann originated few ideas on educational methods, but credit him with being a perceptive reader of educational theorists, especially Pestalozzi, and a keen observer and critic of good teaching. His own ideas were shaped and influenced by the opportunity he had to observe teaching both in Europe and at home. His views on teaching methods were broadened and enriched by his European travels. Even if not an originator of great educational concepts, Mann deserves full recognition for his remarkable ability to identify and select the ideas of theorists and the methods of the best teachers that could be most suitably adapted to the common schools, and for interpreting and popularizing these ideas in his writings and lectures. By such means, he influenced popular education directly and positively, not only in Massachusetts but also in other states and countries.

CHAPTER 5

Preparation of Teachers

In the *First Annual Report of the Board of Education,* as previously noted, Horace Mann listed "the competency of teachers" as one of four matters of cardinal importance to the common schools. He was fully aware that any significant improvement in the public school system depended first of all on obtaining better teachers. The answer, he was convinced, was the establishment of special schools for the training of teachers.

Inferior teachers had contributed in major fashion to the deplorable state of Massachusetts schools when Mann came onto the scene in 1837. There had been a steady decline in the quality of teachers until, as Jonathan Messerli points out, "the ranks were filled largely with young girls, spinsters, former clergymen, farmers, mechanics, and college students." Virtually none of the motley lot had any intention or expectation of making a profession of teaching, but were merely seeking a temporary job pending a search for a more remunerative and prestigious profession or trade, or, in the case of the women, marriage. Then, Mann observed, "having gained the temporary purpose for which they entered upon the business, they abandon it—not merely without regret, but with alacrity."

An inquiry conducted by Mann in 1846 among 2,846 Massachusetts teachers revealed that 1,701 had taught for less than two years and 1,014 for one year or less. It is scarcely surprising, therefore, in view of the general incompetence, lack of training, and absence of any sense of dedication to teaching, that Mann should report, in the same year, more than ninety schools had been closed prematurely, or "broken up" by the insubordination of the students.

The need for training schools for teachers had long been recognized. In Europe the normal school idea was at least 150 years old. Franklin's Academy in Philadelphia had been founded in 1756 partly for the purpose of training teachers. In 1823, the Reverend Samuel R. Hall established at Concord, Vermont, what was probably the first school in America specifically for the training of teachers. Later, in 1830, Hall became principal of a school for preparing teachers at the Andover Academy in Massachusetts, a program which continued in successful operation for five years.

Particularly influential were several reports circulated in Massachusetts describing the teacher-training schools in Prussia. A translation of Victor Cousin's *Report on the State of Public Instruction* was published in newspapers and widely read. Calvin E. Stowe (Harriet Beecher's husband) had been authorized by the state of Ohio to make a study of teacher training in Europe and his *Report on Elementary Education in Europe* was republished and extensively circulated in Massachusetts and other states. A self-appointed missionary for the cause, the Reverend Charles Brooks, Unitarian minister of Hingham, had become enamored with the Prussian system during travels in Germany and gave numerous lectures advocating the creation of normal schools on the same model in America.

Further fuel to the flame was added by a noted Boston clergyman, William E. Channing, speaking to a large and influential audience on February 28, 1837, a few months before Mann accepted the Board of Education post. In an eloquent, impassioned plea for normal schools and better teachers, Channing declared:

We need an institution for the formation of better teachers; and until this step is taken, we can make no important progress. The most crying need in this Commonwealth is the want of accomplished teachers. We boast of our schools, but our schools do comparatively little for want of educated instructors. Without good teaching a school is but a name. An institution for training men to train the young would be a fountain of living waters, sending forth streams to refresh present and future ages. . . .We want better teachers, and more teachers for all classes of society, for rich and poor, for children and adults. . . .We need a new profession or vocation, the object of which shall be to wake up the intellect in those spheres where it is now buried in habitual slumber. . . .The wealth of the community should flow out like water for the employment of such teachers, for enlisting powerful and generous minds in the work of giving impulse to their race.[29]

With such enthusiasm already generated, by the time Horace Mann assumed the Secretaryship of the Board of Education there was mounting sentiment throughout Massachusetts in favor of setting up special schools for the preparation of teachers. Nothing concrete had developed, however, and it was Mann who deserves credit for translating the whole movement into action and bringing about the establishment of the first state-supported normal schools—schools to be owned, supported, and governed by the state for the state's service, contrary to earlier proposals for private institutions with the same object.

The groundwork was laid in the Board of Education's *First Annual Report* in a section written by Governor Edward Everett. Therein it was pointed out that "the arduous and manifold duties of the instructor of youth" could not be well performed without specific preparation for them. Governor Everett continued:

In fact it must be admitted, as the voice of reason and experience, that institutions for the formation of teachers must be established among us, before the all-important work of forming the minds of our children can be performed in the best possible manner, and with the greatest attainable success. . . .In those foreign countries, where the greatest attention has been paid to the work of education, schools for teachers have formed an important feature in their systems, and with the happiest result. . . .The Board cannot but express the sanguine hope, that the time is not far distant when the resources of public or private liberality will be applied in Massachusetts for the foundation of an institution for the formation of teachers, in which the present existing defect will be amply supplied.[30]

The final and deciding factor came to a head on March 10, 1838, when Horace Mann was invited to the home of Edmund Dwight, a prominent member of the Board and wealthy manufacturer. Following extended discussion, Mann was authorized to report that Dwight would contribute $10,000 toward the establishment of schools for preparing teachers, if the legislature would appropriate an equal amount. A joint committee recommended acceptance of the offer, and a resolution was passed —unanimously in the House of Representatives and with a single dissenting vote in the Senate—making the plan effective.

Responsibility for expending the funds appropriated and for organizing the new institutions was turned over to the Board of Education. Since these were pioneer schools, the first of their kind in America, there were no precedents to follow or examples to emulate. Three basic problems had to be resolved immediately: the number and locations of the schools, the selection of suitable teachers, and the planning of a curriculum.

The initial decision was that there should be three schools. Further, it was agreed that the schools could be made most effective by placing them in different areas of the state: one in the northeast, one in the southeast, and a third in the western section. On the other hand, the amount available was inadequate to cover the entire expense of such a plan; the further decision was made, therefore, to place the schools in communities where the cost of buildings and equipment, and other expenses, exclusive of teachers' salaries, would be borne by the communities in which the schools were to be located. No less than thirteen applications, a majority agreeing to meet the conditions, were received by the Board.

Because its application was first to be filed, its situation was favorable, and its citizens offered the most generous donation, Lexington was chosen as the location for a school in the northeastern section of the state. A short while later, Barre in the central region and Bridgewater in the southeast were added. Subsequently, the school at Barre was transferred to Westfield, while the Lexington school was moved to West Newton and later to Framingham, where it still remains. The normal school at Bridgewater has had the longest continuous existence on the same site, dating from its inauguration, September 9, 1840.

The opening of the Lexington school on July 3, 1839, was unimpressive. Attendance was limited to women, and only three girls applied for admission. The small enrollment simply convinced Mann that more exertion was needed to make the program succeed. His faith was vindicated, for soon the student body at Lexington had outgrown the available space, necessitating removal of the school to a larger building at West Newton.

A fortunate choice was made by Mann for the first principal of the Lexington school, Cyrus Peirce of Nantucket, an able teacher and administrator. Peirce's superhuman efforts to insure the success of the enterprise included careful preparation of every lesson he taught, maintenance of a large correspondence, establishment of a model school and supervision of the normal students' teaching, and even janitor service for the school. Students were expected to rise at five o'clock and study for an hour before breakfast. From then on, class sessions as well as study and rest periods filled the day until eight o'clock in the evening.

Entrance to the normal schools was by examination. Applicants for admission had to be sixteen years of age, in good health, and were required to sign a declaration of intention to teach. The entering tests were in reading, writing, orthography, English grammar, geography, and arithmetic. It soon became apparent that a major obstacle to the success of the schools was poor preparation of students. Much time had to be devoted, therefore, to correcting deficiencies of the most elementary nature in the students' background. Another hindrance was the students' inability to remain for more than one semester, though Mann and Peirce maintained that even a month's training would substantially improve a person's ability to teach.

Selection of a course of study for the normal schools was of course a crucial problem for Mann and his associates. The curriculum, it was decided, should be designed specifically to prepare teachers for the common schools, in order to provide a "more thorough and systematic acquaintance with the branches usually taught in common schools," along with other areas of knowledge useful to a teacher. The classical languages, Greek and Latin, were omitted in favor of an introduction to simple geography, grammar, spelling, and arithmetic. A second feature of the program was to teach the "art of imparting instruction to the youthful mind, which will be taught in its principles, and illustrated by opportunity for practice, by means of a model school." A "school of practice," from the beginning an essential feature of teacher-training institutions, was to insure that, as Governor Everett pointed out, "under the principal of the school, the young teacher may have the benefit of actual exercise in the business of instruction." At Lexington, Peirce demonstrated methods of teaching and required the students to teach under his supervision. Thus from the outset, the normal school curriculum included three basic elements: subject matter, methodology of teaching, and practice teaching.

A highly delicate decision had to be reached concerning religious and moral instruction. The Board of Education came out unreservedly for nonsectarian religious teaching. Among the listed subjects of instruction in the normal schools was "The Principles of Piety and Morality, common to all sects of Christians." Further, the Board laid down as a principle that "a portion of the Scriptures shall be daily read."

Only at Lexington was student enrollment restricted to women. The policy was deliberate and in accord with firm convictions held by Horace Mann, a strong advocate of the employment of more women as teachers, especially in the primary grades. Other influential educational leaders of the time were in agreement as to the desirability of recruiting a larger proportion of women for the profession. Mann's principal arguments in support of this belief were that women are better fitted by nature than are men to train and educate young children, they are freer of "vulgar practices and political ambitions," they are "more mild and gentle," have "stronger parental impulses," are "less withdrawn from their employment," "less intent and scheming for future honors and emoluments," and are possessed of "purer morals." A practical consideration, not overlooked by Mann and school governing boards, was that women's salaries were lower and their services could be obtained more cheaply. In any event, after establishment of the normal schools, the percentage of women in the teaching field steadily increased.

In a lecture delivered at the time of his resignation as Secretary of the Board, Mann reiterated his position: "That woman should be the educator of children, I believe to be as much a requirement of nature as that she should be the mother of children. Education, I say emphatically, is woman's work—the domain of her empire, the sceptre of her power, the crown of her glory."

Initially, the normal schools were established for a three-year experimental period. As the time drew to a close, Mann and other friends of the schools had cause to wonder about their future, despite strong legislative support and endorsements by prominent citizens. Political power shifted in 1840, the Democrats won the state house from the Whigs, and the Massachusetts government was experiencing financial woes. The solution offered by the new governor, Marcus Morton, no friend of Mann's, was to "Let retrenchment be a substitute for taxation. If there be any supernumerary officers, or agencies, or commissions not immediately necessary for the public good, abolish them."

From the beginning, opposition to the normal schools had been developing among a variety of dissident elements. The private academies and high schools which had previously enjoyed a monopoly on the preparation of teachers attacked the normal schools as competitors. A majority report of the Committee on Education of the House of Representatives recommended that the bill establishing the normal schools should be rescinded, for such reasons as the following: the schools were too much under French and Prussian influence; they had no apparent advantage over academies and high schools which cost the Commonwealth nothing; attendance at the schools was small; since public schools ran only a few months a year, it was impossible for teaching to become a profession; and there was danger in having all teachers formed after one model. Another source of criticism was sectarian interests, which disapproved of the schools because they did not teach religion and accused them further of being under Unitarian influence.

But forces for the defense began to rally around. A minority report of the Committee on Education was submitted to the House of Representatives calling attention to the devotion of members of the Board of Education who served without pay, to the small salary of the Board's Secretary, to the private benevolence which had made the normal schools possible, and to their excellent programs. Certain human considerations were also emphasized in the minority report: the contracts with teachers, the upset in the lives of the students, and the breach of faith with the boarding-house keepers and friends in the towns where the schools were located, who had pledged their support. Horace Mann, ex-Governor Everett, and Henry Barnard, influential educational leader from Connecticut, worked privately among the members of the legislature. The outcome was that a small majority against the Board and the normal schools was turned into a substantial majority in their favor. The significance of the victory was thus described by Henry Barnard:

The friends of public schools, and of special institutions for the qualification and improvement of teachers, and of state supervision of the great interest of education, in every state, owe a large debt of gratitude to those men who achieved a triumph for the Board of Education, the normal schools and Mr. Mann, in the legislature of Massachusetts, in 1840. Defeat there and then . . . would have changed the whole condition of public instruction in this country, for a half century, if not forever.[31]

Full confirmation came two years later, as Mann wrote on March 3, 1842: "The brightest days which have ever shone upon our cause were yesterday and to-day. Yesterday resolves passed the House for granting $6,000 per year for three years to the Normal schools." State appropriations were again renewed in 1845, after which opposition to the normal schools practically disappeared. In the winter of 1844-45, a group of friends of popular education met in Boston and agreed to donate $5,000 for normal school buildings, provided their gift would be matched by the legislature. The condition was met and in 1846 a building at Bridgewater and another at Westfield were dedicated—the first to be built by the state exclusively for normal school purposes.

In his *Twelfth* and final *Annual Report* Horace Mann reaffirmed his faith in normal schools, declaring that:

On a careful review and inspection of all that has been done, within the past twelve years, to improve the common schools of Massachusetts, and of the special instrumentalities by which these improvements have been effected, I cannot refrain from assigning the first place, in adaptedness and in efficiency, to our state normal schools. . . .

Common schools will never prosper without normal schools. As well might we expect to have coats without a tailor, and hats without a hatter, and watches without a watchmaker, and houses without a carpenter or mason, as to have an adequate supply of teachers without normal schools.[32]

With the normal schools apparently well launched, Horace

Mann was ready to try another device for the improvement of teaching. It was obvious that the facilities of the normal school were insufficient to reach more than a fraction of the teachers in the Massachusetts schools, who then numbered more than six thousand. Many teachers, in any case, could not afford to attend a normal school for a full term. The answer proposed by Mann was a variation of normal school training: bring the schools to the teachers in the form of teacher institutes. The idea was not original with Mann. Several years previously, Henry Barnard had conducted the first such county teachers' institute in Hartford, Connecticut, and shortly thereafter a number of the larger counties of New York adopted the scheme. Teachers' institutes had been held in Ohio, also, as aids in training programs.

Mann modeled the Massachusetts institutes after those in New York, stating, "We have borrowed her system of district school libraries. She has borrowed our system of normal schools. Let us now adopt the system of teachers' institutes, which she has projected." Again private funds were needed to demonstrate the value of the plan to a doubtful legislature and again Mann's friend Edmund Dwight gave him financial as well as moral support. With a contribution of $1,000, in the summer of 1845 Mann organized four institutes, each two weeks in length, at Pittsfield, Fitchburg, Bridgewater, and Chatham. The attendance in each was limited to 100 teachers or other persons wishing to teach.

The teachers' institutes have been described as "little normal schools in embryonic form." In arranging programs for them, Mann quite realistically recognized the teachers' limited education. The instructors were directed to review arithmetic, stressing the fundamental rules and their methods of proof, to study geography and to conduct spelling drills, and even show how to write a simple letter. In addition, teaching demonstrations were held; as Mann reported, "observations on the best methods of teaching each branch were interspersed in all the exercises pertaining to that branch."

The success of the venture was immediately evident. After the first year, the legislature was easily persuaded to appropriate $2,500 annually for the support of the institutes, which thus became a regular feature of the Massachusetts program for improving common school instruction. Though gradually outmoded, as superior training opportunities were provided, in their day the institutes were a stimulating influence and helped to demonstrate the need for normal school education.

In summarizing Horace Mann's notable contributions to teacher education, it should be observed in the first place that he convinced the citizens of Massachusetts of the fact that the success of the common schools was primarily dependent upon trained teachers. The normal schools which he was instrumental in founding set the pattern of study generally followed by teacher-training institutions since his day: knowledge of the subjects to be taught, methods of teaching and school management, and practice teaching. American normal schools proliferated after the Civil War and those in other states benefited directly from the pioneering work done in Massachusetts under Mann's guidance.

CHAPTER 6

Books and Libraries

The effectiveness of the common schools in Massachusetts was vitally affected, Horace Mann was convinced, by the nonuniformity of textbooks and and the lack of school libraries. Immediately after his appointment as Secretary of the Board of Education, he turned his attention to these aspects of the educational system.

The *First Annual Report* is full of scathing criticism of what Mann describes as "a public evil of great magnitude in the multiplicity and diversity of elementary books"; he adds, "They crowd the market and infest the schools." Superiority was claimed by the publishers for some books because they made learning easy and others because they made learning difficult. Books differed even in basic information, as a consequence of which "By a change of books a child is often obliged to unlearn what he had laboriously acquired before." Efforts by school committees to standardize selections were resisted by the parents, who objected to the expense of purchasing new books; hence the chaotic situation worsened instead of improving. Pupils in classes could not recite together, for "If eight or ten scholars [students], in geography for instance, have eight or ten different books, as has sometimes happened, instead of one recitation for all, there must be eight or ten recitations. Thus the teacher's time is crumbled into dust and dissipated. . . .This irretrievable loss is incurred merely because parents will not agree to procure the best books."[33]

The failure to regulate textbook selection, Mann points out, "holds out a standing invitation to every book-pedlar and speculator to foist in his books, which may be new, or they may be books whose sheets have been printed for years, but garnished with a new title-page bearing a recent date." In many instances, certain texts were used because the teacher himself studied the books when in school, or was accustomed to teach from them.

Of the 300 towns in the Commonwealth, Mann reports, at least 100 neglected to prescribe textbooks for the common schools, despite the fact that the law enjoined the town school committees "to direct what books shall be used in the several schools" in their communities. Instead of saving money, as some shortsighted parents thought, "There cannot be a doubt, that the aggregate expense of books for any given number of years, will be much greater in towns where the committees are thwarted by the parents in the discharge of this duty, than in towns where it is duly performed."

The complete unsuitability for children of the readers in current use also met with Mann's censure. Many, he felt, were "too elevated for the scholars," since "It seems generally to have been the object of the compilers of these books, to cull the most profound and brilliant passages, contained in a language, in which the highest efforts of learning, talent and genius have been embalmed." The choice of "abstruse and recondite subjects, tasking the acuteness of practiced logicians" could have but one end result: "Using incomprehensible reading books draws after it the inevitable consequences of bad reading."[34]

No less objectionable in Mann's view was the heterogeneity of subject matter in the readers. No subject was treated in any except the most sketchy fashion and logical relationships among successive selections were nonexistent. Ludicrous examples are cited by Mann from a text in use in some of the schools. A humorous essay, "On the head-dress of ladies," was followed by another entitled "On a future state of eternal happiness or perdition," after which came Milton's "Creation of the world," "The facetious history of John Gilpin," Thompson's "Hymn to the Deity," Merrick's "Chameleon," Blair's "Sermon on the death of Christ," and Lord Chesterfield's "Speech on pensions."[35]

During his first year as Secretary, Mann received numerous requests "to recommend class books for the schools, or to state what books were considered best by the Board, or by myself." Since neither the Secretary nor the Board had any legal authority in the matter, no opinions were expressed. In a circular to the local school committees, however, Mann asked: "Would it be generally acceptable to the friends of Education in your town, to have the Board of Education recommend books for the use of the schools?" The response was mixed. Replies from twenty towns declared that such a recommendation would be unacceptable. On the other hand, the Secretary found, "the friends of Education in towns containing more than seven-eighths of the population of the State, are in favor of having the Board of Education *recommend* books for the use of the Schools."

At the conclusion of his *Second Annual Report,* noting "the alarming deficiency of moral and religious instruction in the schools," the Secretary stated his belief that the deficiency "could only be explained by supposing, that school committees, whose duty it is to prescribe school books, had not found any books at once, expository of the doctrines of revealed religion, and, also free from such advocacy of the 'tenets' of particular sects of Christians, as brought them, in their opinion, within the scope of the legal prohibition."[36] The unavailability of "proper manuals" led the committees to exclude any books on the subject.

Several years later, in his *Fifth Annual Report,* Mann again deplored the failure to achieve uniformity in textbook selection, and repeated his admonition that "uniformity and economy go hand in hand, while the evil of diversity brings with it the evil of a wasteful expenditure." One of the consequences, too, was "a serious inconvenience to teachers," who could not afford to purchase personal copies of the variety of texts owned by the children and therefore were often forced to hear recitations without having in their hands the particular texts from which the recitations were presented.[37]

Mann did not review the schoolbook situation again until his *Tenth Annual Report,* near the end of his term as Secretary. It is apparent that a certain degree of progress had been achieved in the interim, though problems remained because of the Board of Education's lack of specific authority and the decentralization of control among a multitude of local committees. His report is used by Mann as an occasion for calling further attention to the legal requirements and responsibilities of school committees under the law. The chief provisions of the law as revised to 1847, it was noted, were the following: The committee was to prescribe what books were to be used in the schools; a copy of the list was to be placed in the hands of each teacher before the opening of the school; the committee *may* direct what books shall be used in various classes; after the list has been prepared and placed in the hands of the teacher and parents, there was to be "a virtual exclusion of all other text books from the school"; it was the duty of parents to supply their children with copies of books pre-scribed by the committee, but in the event of their failure to do so, the students were to be provided with books by the committee at the expense of the town.

Fewer frustrations and more success were met with by Mann in another bookish area: district school libraries. Nearly all of the *Third Annual Report* is devoted to the improvement of libraries and the effect of reading on the formation of character.[38]

Certain preliminary inquiries were made by the Secretary prior to his crusade for good school libraries. Mann pens a paean of praise for the ability to read, noting "the vast amount of knowl-edge which can be acquired through the medium of intelligent reading" and suggesting that "with this ability. . .we are endued with a power of being present, at pleasure, with the distant and the past,—we can visit, with the rapidity of thought, any nation or spot on the surface of the globe, and become the coeval of time, and a contemporary with the great names and events of all his-toric eras." But then, the grim realities of the situation are recog-nized: "after the rising generation have acquired habits of intel-ligent reading in our schools, *what shall they read?*—for with no books to read, the power of reading will be useless." A crucial question then is: "What books are accessible to the great mass of the children in the State?"

Since sound and permanent reading habits are normally formed at an early age and the environment is a fundamental factor, Mann asks what books were available in the homes. The answers were discouraging. Among the agricultural population, books were ordinarily limited to the Scriptures and a few school-books; in the houses of such professional men as ministers, lawyers, and physicians were to be found small professional li-braries accompanied by some miscellaneous works; in the houses of religious persons, a few religious books in harmony with the owner's faith; in the homes of the wealthy "some useful and instructive books," though sometimes "unfortunately united with a love of display" which produced "a few elegantly bound annuals, and novels of recent emission." In the majority of homes there would be found a few books of a most miscellaneous character, "books which had found their way thither, rather by chance than by design, and ranging in their character between very good and very bad." Rarely included were any works dealing with government, economics and statistics, ethics and philosophy, the application of science to agriculture and the useful arts, American colonial history, and education, or general encyclopedias.

Having painted a generally dismal picture of the state of home libraries, Mann turned next to public libraries, and tried to ascertain the following facts: "What number of public libraries exist; how many volumes they contain, 'and what are their general character, scope and tendency; how many persons have access to them, or,—which is the most material point,—how many persons do *not* have access to them;—and finally, how many of the books are adapted to prepare children to be free citizens and men, fathers and mothers, even in the most limited signification of those vastly comprehensive words."

Simultaneously with a questionnaire sent to school committees on the subject of public libraries, Mann inquired about another type of institution, lyceums or mechanics' institutes, which had recently become popular in Massachusetts, conducting popular lectures on literary and scientific subjects and in some instances possessing libraries and reading rooms.

The *Third Annual Report* presents detailed statistics of Mann's findings, county by county. More than one-half of all the books in the state were in Boston, though only one-tenth of the city's population had access to them. Considering the state as a whole, approximately 100,000 of the total population of 700,000 had a right of access to libraries of any type. Among institutional libraries, Harvard University held the largest collection (50,000 volumes) followed by Amherst College with 13,000 volumes, and the American Antiquarian Society Library with 12,000 volumes, but the general public was excluded from such institutions. "The aggregate number of volumes in the public libraries of all kinds,

in the State," Mann reported, "is about three hundred thousand."
Nearly 100 towns, one-third of the state's total, possessed no
town, social, or district school library.

Particularly distressing to Mann was the unequal distribution
of library resources over the state: "a few, deep, capacious reser-
voirs, surrounded by broad wastes. It has long been a common
remark, that many persons read too much; but here we have
proof, how many thousands read too little. For the poor man and
the laboring man, the art of printing seems hardly yet to have
been discovered."

Along with the matter of quantity, Mann was interested in the
quality of the collections available, especially their suitability for
children and young people. "Almost all the answers concur in the
opinion," he states, "that the contents of the libraries are not
adapted to the intellectual and moral wants of the young. . . .With
very few exceptions, the books were written for adults, for persons of some maturity of mind, and possessed, already, of a
considerable fund of information." A numerous category was
histories. "And how little," exclaims Mann, "do these books contain, which is suitable for children! How little do they record but
the destruction of human life, and the activity of those misguided
energies, which have hitherto almost baffled the beneficent in-
tentions of nature for human happiness. Descriptions of battles,
sackings of cities, and the captivity of nations, follow each other
with the quickest movement, and in an endless succession."[39]

Another class of books of which Mann was highly critical,
though for different reasons, was novels and similar works which
he lumped together as "fictions," "light reading," "trashy works,"
"ephemeral," or "bubble literature," a variety that was becoming
increasingly popular during his time. Here was definitely a blind
side to Mann's literary tastes. His principal objection to fictional
works was that their object was "mere amusement, as contradistinguished from instruction in the practical concerns of life; as
contradistinguished from those intellectual and moral impulses,
which turn the mind, both while reading and after the book is
closed, to observation and comparison and reflection upon the
great realities of existence."[40] Thus, he was reluctant to include
the fictional writings of his wife's brother-in-law, Nathaniel

Hawthorne, in the list of books recommended for school libraries, or Richard Henry Dana, Jr.'s *Two Years Before the Mast* without extensive rewriting to make the work of practical value.

Mann's survey of all types of libraries in the Commonwealth, done in 1839, revealed "Only about fifty common-school libraries exist in the three thousand districts of the state." The campaign by the Board and its Secretary on behalf of such libraries began early. In the *First Annual Report,* it is stated that "The subject of district school libraries is deemed of very great importance by the Board." The foundation was laid by an 1837 legislative enactment authorizing an expenditure by each district of thirty dollars the first year and ten each succeeding year for the establishment of libraries. The Board suggested that "it would be highly desirable that each school-house should be furnished with a case and shelves suitable for the proper arrangement and safe keeping of books."

But despite the pious hope, it became obvious that there was little activity on the library front. In its *Second Annual Report,* the Board again commented on the subject, noting that "scarce any of the districts of the Commonwealth have as yet availed themselves of the authority granted by the act of 12th of April, 1837." Even when established, the school libraries were handicapped by the unavailability of suitable books to stock them. At first, the Board was unwilling to intervene, preferring to leave it to "the enterprise of intelligent publishers" to correct the situation. The Board recognized, however, that a principal reason for the failure of the districts to take advantage of the school library law was "the difficulty of making the selection:—a difficulty of considerable magnitude, when but a small sum is to be expended, and it is necessary to send to some distant place for a supply of books."

Accordingly, after considerable debate, the Board decided to seize the bull by the horns, in order to remove this obstacle, and "to recommend to some respectable publishing house to issue from the press a collection of works as a common school library, to consist of two series; the one adapted for the use of children, the other for a maturer class of readers." The proposal was accepted by Marsh, Capen, & Lyon of Boston, who agreed to execute the series in conformity with guidelines furnished by the Board, but at the expense and risk of the publisher. An important stipulation was that "Each book in the series is to be submitted to the inspection of every member of the Board, and no work is to be recommended, but on their unanimous approval." It would remain optional with the school districts whether to purchase the books recommended by the Board, though since "many of the most distinguished writers of our country" were to contribute to the series, widespread acceptance was anticipated.

Actually, Massachusetts was not the first state to organize school libraries. The progenitor appears to have been Governor DeWitt Clinton of New York, an enlightened friend of public education, who recommended such libraries in his annual message to the legislature in 1827. It was not until 1835, however, that the New York legislature authorized school districts to impose a tax, not exceeding twenty dollars for the first year and ten dollars a year thereafter, for the purchase of libraries. Within fifteen years the school library movement had placed 1,600,000 volumes within the reach of New York's school children.

Horace Mann acknowledged that he had been inspired by the success of the New York program, just as New York had learned from Massachusetts' pioneer normal schools. It was at his urging that the Board moved to breathe life into the 1837 law. As seen by Mann, the financial support specified for school libraries was trifling, but in its long-range implications, the law was hardly second in importance to the 1647 act creating the common schools of the state. The schools have only begun their work, he insisted, when they have taught children to read; it is equally their duty to give them a taste for good reading and critical judgment for determining what is worth reading.

The series of books issued by the Boston publisher was divided between "The Massachusetts Primary School Library" and "The Massachusetts Common School Library," each consisting of fifty volumes. The first, prepared especially for children, sold for forty cents a volume, and the latter, for more mature readers, for seventy-five cents. The price and style of binding were fixed by the Board. More important, the books were written by individuals "distinguished for learning, judgement, and moral excellence," who were members of different political parties and religious denominations.

The first ten volumes announced for publication were the

following: Washington Irving's *Life of Columbus* (1 volume), Paley's *Natural Theology* (2 volumes), *Lives of Eminent Individuals Celebrated in American History* (3 volumes), and Henry Duncan's *The Sacred Philosophy of the Seasons* (4 volumes).

Certainly no one could accuse the Board or the publisher of corrupting youthful minds by light reading in the initial selections. Listed for later publication were Upham's *Life of Washington*, Wayland's *The Pursuit of Knowledge Under Difficulties*, Story's *A Familiar Exposition of the Constitution of the United States*, Spark's *Selections from the Writings of Franklin*, Potter's *Science and the Arts*, Robbins' *Christianity and Knowledge*, Burton's *The Lord of the Soil*, Buel's *The Farmer's Companion*, Mrs. Embury's *Biographical Sketches of Distinguished Females*, works on human physiology, chemistry, astronomy, natural philosophy, the useful arts, geology and mineralogy, American trees and plants, political economy, statistics, and some twenty-five other works of varying interest and difficulty. Among the authors, probably Washington Irving, Nathaniel Hawthorne, and Maria Edgeworth would be the only names readily recognized today. The announced purpose of the series was to "furnish youth with suitable works for perusal during their leisure hours; works that will interest as well as instruct them, and of such character that they will turn to them when it is desirable to unbend from the studies of the school room."[41]

What Mann and the Board were seeking, with more or less success, was the creation of a literature adapted to the understanding of child readers. This was a new concept. Even great artists of previous eras had depicted children as miniature adults, and authors and publishers were under the same delusion. Literature written for children most commonly had a religious flavor, designed to instill in them a desire for pious lives. Sunday school books were a flourishing branch of publishing in Mann's time, and he was resolved that "The Board would not become instrumental in introducing the American Sunday School library into our Common Schools."

It was this determination which almost immediately involved Mann in violent dispute with Frederick A. Packard, Editorial Secretary of the Sunday School Union, characterized by Louise Hall Tharp as "one of the most persistent, unscrupulous and sharp-dealing book agents that ever lived!" The controversy began when Packard wrote to Mann to inquire whether John Stevens Cabot Abbott's *The Child at Home,* one of about a dozen volumes for children published by the Union, would be accepted into the school district libraries of the state. The story centered around a six-year-old child who had managed to get himself involved in a childish prank. As the narrative continued, Mann was shocked to read: "But we must not forget that there is a day of most solemn judgement near at hand. When you die, your body will be wrapped in a shroud, placed in the coffin and buried in the grave. . . .How awful must be the scene when you enter the eternal world!. . .You will see God seated upon that majestic throne. . . .The angels will see your sin and disgrace. . . .The Savior will look upon you in his displeasure. . . .You must hear the awful sentence, 'Depart from me into everlasting fire!' "

Mann replied to Packard at once, with more heat than tact: "I cannot hesitate a moment in saying that it would not be tolerated in this state as a District School library book. . . .There is scarcely anything in the book which presents the character of God in an admirable or loving aspect," adding that it would be better to have no libraries at all than one composed of such books as the one proposed, and also that the law forbade the use of sectarian books. Further efforts by Packard to sell the Union's books for the school libraries were futile. Soon thereafter he vented his anger against Mann and the Board at a meeting in New Bedford attended by Sunday school workers of the state, and published a series of anonymous letters attacking Mann and condemning "godless" schools. The running fight continued for several years, with revenge apparently Packard's chief motive, as he dropped active promotion of the Sunday School Union's books.

Even closer home for Mann was opposition within the Board of Education itself to the district school libraries. Edward A. Newton, banker and prominent Episcopalian from Pittsfield, was one of eight persons originally appointed to the Board when it was created in 1837. An ultraconservative aristocrat by heredity and training, Newton was basically out of sympathy with the common school movement, and most particularly with the decision to ban sectarian instruction from the schools. The Board's action in approving the arrangement for publishing books suitable for school libraries was strongly opposed by Newton, who saw the project as evidence of further secularization of education. Following his inability to persuade the Board to rescind its action on the common school library, his resignation was tendered to Governor Everett. Thenceforth, Newton joined Packard and other critics as an active enemy of Mann and the Board. The general sentiment toward Newton's departure appears to have been well expressed in a letter from a member of the Northampton school committee, who wrote Mann: "His appointment was decidedly the greatest blunder our Governor has made and I trust that some pains will be taken to save him from another similar mistake. In selecting a person to fill the vacancy reference should be had quite as much to the character of the candidate's heart as to his head—especially to his social tendencies."

Keen insight was shown by one of Horace Mann's first biographers, B. A. Hinsdale, writing in 1898. Commenting on the district school library project, Hinsdale's judgment was that:

In their time, these libraries supplied a great number of people —children, youth and adults—with a store of excellent reading matter that, otherwise, they could not have enjoyed. They were an anticipation, no doubt vague and unsatisfactory, of the idea now so well defined, that the library is an invaluable auxiliary to the school. They prepared the way for the free public library, which has come to be an inseparable adjunct of a good school system, and a necessity to every progressive American community that is large enough to support it. Horace Mann therefore made no mistake when he pleaded for the children's library with an eloquence equal to that with which he pleaded for the teachers' Normal school.[42]

CHAPTER 7

Education for Health

Not least among Horace Mann's pioneering efforts in the educational field was his work in health and physical education. His deep interest in an area hitherto almost completely neglected in the schools may be attributed first to his own chronic ill health, which made him acutely aware of the importance of physical well-being, and perhaps, second, to his belief in phrenology, which identified mind as body and promoted concepts of physical education and training. As Robert Clifton Whittemore comments, in his *Makers of the American Mind,* "As we contemplate the major role of physical education in our schools and colleges today, we would do well to remember that it mostly began with phrenology."

Also reinforcing Mann's awareness of the physical side of education was the deplorable condition of many schoolhouses when he became Secretary of the Board of Education. After personally examining about 800 buildings and collecting information on 1,000 others, Mann declared that the buildings were usually a menace to the health of the children and a disgrace to the communities in which they were located. "I am convinced," he states, in the *Third Annual Report,* "that there is no other class of buildings within our limits, erected either for the permanent or the temporary residence of our native population, so inconvenient, so uncomfortable, so dangerous to health by their construction within, or so unsightly and repulsive to their appearance without."[43] Children were forced to bend their spines for six hours a day as they sat like so many birds perched on a backless pine bench, built too high for their feet to reach the floor. The ventilation was equally appalling, ranging from arctic to tropical temperatures, depending upon where the pupils sat with relation to the fireplace or wood-burning heater.

To substantiate his critical judgment of the state of the Commonwealth's school buildings, Mann cites a case study by "a highly respectable physician," who had investigated the actual results of bad internal arrangements and of bad locations for schoolhouses upon the health of the students. Statistics were maintained upon the relative amount of illness suffered by the children during a given period of time in two schools. The schools were selected on account of their proximity to each other, they enrolled approximately the same number of students, and the children came from the same types of families. One house was dry and well ventilated, the other damp and impossible to ventilate satisfactorily. In the latter school four times as many children lost time because of illness, and for seven times as many days, as in the first school. From this study, Mann contended that no one "can remain sceptical in regard to the connexion between good health and pure air."

The *Sixth Annual Report* has been described as a "Dissertation on the Study of Physiology in the Schools." In essence, the report is a practical treatise upon the applications of physiology. "No person is qualified to have the care of children for a single day," Mann asserts, "who is ignorant of the leading principles of physiology," in which he included hygiene. To hammer the point home, he adds, "Graduates of colleges and of theological seminaries, who would be ashamed if they did not know that Alexander's horse was named Bucephalus, or had not read Middleton's octavo volume upon the Greek article, are often profoundly ignorant of the great laws which God has impressed upon their physical frame, and which, under penalty of forfeiting life and usefulness, He has commanded them to know and obey."[44]

Irony can be detected in Mann's comparison between the way in which men raise horses and cows and their own children. The farm animals are bred to be healthy and strong, while the "children are puny, distempered, and have chronic diseases." Except for children born with hereditary weaknesses or who suffer crippling accidents, the state of a person's health in later years "depends upon his treatment of himself, or rather, upon the treatment of those who manage his infancy and childhood, and create his habits for him." To Mann, personal physical health was a moral duty and in his view, "a person without high health is just as much at war with nature as a guilty soul is at war with the spirit of God."

Holding such firm convictions on health education, Mann mandatorily included the subject in the curriculum of the newly established normal schools. The journal of Mary Swift, a student in the first class of the first state normal school, at Lexington, notes that "physiology" was one of the required courses. During the third week of the course, Miss Swift brought out in her diary a point which apparently was being stressed in the instruction, that is, the teacher's own health:

> There are certain qualities which are very desirable to a teacher. . . .The first is health—some leave other occupations as too laborious and teach school, thinking that the trials of the schoolroom are much less than those of any other station. Health is essential to the teacher, not only on his own account but for the sake of his pupils. To the sick, every trial is doubled. Some suffering bad health are better teachers than those enjoying good, but if the same person were possessed with health, he would be probably a much better teacher.

The principal of the Lexington Normal School, Cyrus Peirce, repeatedly urged upon the students the necessity of taking exercise daily, and set aside an hour each morning to be devoted to that purpose. The course at Lexington covered "preventive medicine," so far as it was known at the time, as well as health instruction. It was "taught in no routine fashion," again according to Mary Swift. The textbook for the course was written by Andrew Combe, Mann's friend and adviser, an Edinburgh physician.

If Mann's *Sixth Annual Report,* to be issued four years later, had been available when the Lexington school opened, it too, could have served as a textbook. The report's more than 100 pages of discussion contain a comprehensive treatment of health topics. An editor of Mann's writings, Lawrence A. Cremin, is somewhat critical of the content, pointing out that, "As is frequently the case with Mann's scientific commentaries, fact is liberally interspersed with fiction," but, "Nonetheless, the over-all effect of the report was certainly beneficial at a time when even the most elementary rules of health were unknown to most people."

Mann displays all the zeal of a missionary in the introductory sections of his report, apparently believing that a part of his task was to educate the public on the significance of health study and practice. He begins by asserting that "The study of Human Physiology,—by which I mean both the Laws of Life, and Hygiene or the rules and observances by which health can be preserved and promoted,—has claims so superior to every other [subject in the curriculum] and, at the same time, so little regarded or understood by the community, that I shall ask the indulgence of the Board, while I attempt to vindicate its title to the first rank in our schools, after the elementary branches."

Mann then proceeds to cite some distressing statistics: nearly one-fourth of the human race, even in civilized communities, die before the age of one year, and before the age of twenty, one-half of the people of the world have died. Further, a vast percentage of those who survive are afflicted by diseases and infirmities. Sickness, in turn, breeds poverty, which breeds crime. Many human disabilities are preventable, according to "eminent physicians," who informed Mann that at least one-half of "the suffering and early death inflicted upon mankind proceeds from ignorance,—from sheer ignorance,—of facts and principles" which every parent should know.

A skeptic, no doubt satirically, asked Mann whether he would have all public schools turned into medical schools and all children educated as physicians. In reply, Mann makes a useful distinction: "The *Laws of Health and Life* are comparatively few and simple. Every person is capable of understanding them. Every child in the State, before arriving at the age of eighteen years, might acquire a competent knowledge of them, and of the reasons on which they are founded. The profession of medicine, on the other hand, is mainly conversant with the *Laws of Diseases,*" a far more complex and difficult field.

The most practical instrument available for the transmission and diffusion of knowledge about health care and the prevention of disease, Mann believed, was the common schools. It was only through the schools that virtually all children could be reached.

The "higher seminaries of learning" were unsuitable for the purpose, since they were attended by a small portion of the youth, their curricula were crowded, and females were excluded from colleges and universities.

After six years during which he "visited schools in every section of the Commonwealth, seaboard and inland, city and country," Mann noted striking physical differences between country and city children. The children in rural areas and small towns had "double the bodily energy, the vital force, the stamina of constitution, which belong to the children of cities and of crowded towns." Their bodies, limbs, and muscles were more fully developed, giving them greater vigor and endurance. "On the other hand," Mann found, "the children bred in cities excel in sprightliness and vivacity. . . .Their perceptions are quicker, and their power of commanding more readily both themselves and their attainments, greatly superior."

Mann argued against too intense concentration on class work by the children. In nine-tenths of the schools which he visited the custom prevailed of allowing a ten-minute recess in three-hour sessions, even for children below seven or eight years of age, "though every physiologist or physician knows, that for every forty-five or fifty minutes' confinement in the schoolroom, all children under those ages, should have at least the remaining fifteen or ten minutes of the hour for exercise in the open air."

Disregard of common-sense rules for physical comfort and health was by no means confined to schoolhouse construction, Mann observed. Similarly, there was little attention paid to proper ventilation in courthouses, lecture rooms, churches, sleeping apartments, canal boats, and steamboats. Equally neglected, both for children and adults, was the matter of diet, according to Mann, who emphasized the importance of nutrition in children's growth and warned against overindulgence in any "confectionary or sweetmeats."

Concerning exercise, an essential principle suggested by Mann was regularity—not something to be indulged in once a week or once a month, or to be crowded into a short vacation. Efforts "to promote health by means of exercise which, from its untimeliness or severity," he remarks, "is sure to inflict greater evils than it was intended to avert." Fresh air, exercise, and diet, if they are to contribute to a vigorous life, "depend upon proportion, adaptation, adjustment."

Some resistance to the idea of health education appears to have been met by Mann among fatalists and believers in predestination. Certain individuals, he found, attributed disease to accident or chance or to some occult or remote cause beyond human control. Some believed diseases to be judgments directly inflicted by Heaven upon the body for offences committed against moral law. Still others "suppose pain and untimely bereavement to be a part of the inevitable lot of humanity, designed to test the strength of our confidence in the goodness of the Creator"—in brief, that "our destiny is fixed irrespective of our conduct." Needless to note, such arguments were rejected by Mann, who maintained that providence permits man to help shape his own fate.

Successful careers are built on physical vigor, Mann's argument continued: "Soundness of health is preliminary to the highest success in any pursuit. In every industrial avocation it is an indispensable element; and the highest intellectual eminence can never be reached without it. It exerts a powerful influence over feelings, temper and disposition, and through these upon moral character." It is sheer irony and well-nigh incredible, therefore, Mann writes, that "the means of acquiring vigor, quickness, endurance, have been sought for, not by the clergyman, the lawyer, the artist, the cultivator of letters, the mother; but by the wrestler, the buffoon, the runner, the opera-dancer. There are ten professors of Pugilism in our community, to one of Physical Education in our seminaries of learning."

Hopeful that his eloquent pleas for health education in the common schools had convinced members of the Board, teachers, parents, and the general public, Mann devotes the last sixty pages of the *Sixth Annual Report* to a detailed review of physiology in all its aspects, as currently known or understood, examining one by one the vital organs and bodily functions. From this analysis, he concludes that "the health, vigor, and longevity of the human family are almost entirely dependent upon three things: 1. A sufficient quantity of wholesome and nutritious food, well prepared before it is sent into the stomach. 2. The "due vitalization of the blood in the lungs" (requiring pure air and active exercise). 3.

"Personal cleanliness. . .of the whole surface of the body."

Never having been trained in the medical profession and therefore with limited opportunity "to become acquainted with the laws of health and life," Horace Mann conceded that his views might have contained errors, but there was no shadow of doubt in his mind about the importance of the message: that the study of hygiene and physiology should have a top priority in the public schools. He brings his report to a close with a resounding affirmation of this conviction:

the greatest happiness and the greatest usefulness can never be attained, without that soundness of physical organization which confers the powers of endurance, and that uninterrupted enjoyment of health which ransoms the whole of our time and means from sickness and its expenditures. In the great work of education, then, our physical condition, if not the first step in point of importance, is the first in the order of time.[45]

Mann's continued concern for physical education is evidenced by his twelfth and final report as Secretary, in which he devotes eleven pages to the subject. In general, the points discussed in this farewell statement repeat the arguments presented in the *Sixth Annual Report* and other early reports and articles. The conclusion is reiterated that the common school is the most suitable, indeed the only, agency for "the diffusion of sanitary intelligence." Human physiology should be considered a fundamental branch of study, every teacher should be familiar with its leading principles and of "their applications to the varying circumstances of life," and school committees ought regularly to examine the older classes in the schools upon the subject. "And, as the result and reward of all," Mann promises, "a race of men and women, loftier in stature, firmer in structure, fairer in form, and better able to perform the duties and bear the burdens of life, would revisit the earth. . . . Just in proportion as the laws of health and life were discovered and obeyed, would pain, disease, insanity, and untimely death, cease from among men."

Through Horace Mann's encouragement and stimulation, Massachusetts, in 1850, became the first state to require by law physiology and hygiene as a compulsory subject in all the schools of the Commonwealth. The preparation of classroom teachers in this subject was likewise required by legislative enactment the same year. Thus, Massachusetts became the forerunner for teaching health and physical education in the public schools, a trend which later spread to institutions of higher education. The recognition of health education as an essential and integral part of the curriculum was a direct outgrowth of Mann's educational philosophy.

CHAPTER 8

Sectarian Snipings

Ten years before Horace Mann's appointment as Secretary of the Board of Education, the Massachusetts legislature had enacted legislation barring sectarian teaching from the public schools. The teaching of the principles of Christianity and the Bible, without sectarian bias or interpretation, however, was specifically encouraged. Mann's own beliefs were completely in harmony with the law which was on the statute books when he took office. He was convinced that the introduction of sectarian disputes would destroy the whole common school movement.

Some understanding of the religious situation and its background in New England before and during Mann's time is needed to appreciate the problems with which the Secretary was immediately confronted. The Puritans' principal motivation for emigrating to the New World was to be free to practice their religious dogmas without let or hindrance. For generations their lives were built around the church and in effect a theocracy had been erected in Massachusetts. Public schools had been founded early in the Commonwealth, but for more than 150 years afterward religious instruction was given in them without question and as a matter of course, because the colony was practically homogeneous in its religious beliefs.

By the beginning of the nineteenth century, however, the monolithic structure had begun to crack. Puritan Congregationalism had split three ways—a division which had begun as early as 1734, with Jonathan Edwards as leader in the "Great Awakening." The three parties were the Calvinists, divided into two schools, the "Old Calvinists" and the "New Lights," and the "Liberals," who rejected Calvinism. The "Old Calvinists" held tenaciously to John Calvin's historic teachings, the chief tenets of which assumed the absolute sovereignty of God, the belief that human nature is totally depraved, the idea that man's only hope of salvation is an arbitrarily bestowed grace, the Trinity as inseparable in nature, the divinity and redemption of Jesus Christ, and a view of the Scriptures as the direct, dictated word of God.

Even more extreme doctrines were preached by the "New Light" school, also known as "Strict Calvinists" or "Consistent Calvinists," originating with Jonathan Edwards and carried on by Samuel Hopkins and Nathanael Emmons (Mann's minister). The "New Lights" held not only that man was totally depraved but also that any attempt to use any "means of Grace" to propitiate a vengeful God, to seek one's own salvation, was simply a manifestation of selfishness and self-love, and therefore sinful. Many souls were foreordained to be eternally doomed, regardless of individual will or effort. The consequences of such a doctrine when applied to education were incompatible with everything for which Horace Mann stood, and throughout his career he felt compelled to attack the theological principles on which it was based.

The Liberal Congregationalists were opposed to the creeds preached by both schools of orthodox Calvinism. The Liberals claimed that the Bible does not teach the doctrine of the Trinity, they stressed the humanity of Christ, and they rejected the doctrine of human depravity, implying that regeneration is unnecessary and that the divine forces in man must be given an opportunity to develop through education and training to insure his salvation.

Other dissenting groups, too, were steadily encroaching on the ground long held by the established church. The Baptists, Methodists, Episcopalians, Universalists, Quakers, and Roman Catholics had survived fierce persecution, and were now playing an increasingly important role in the religious life of the Bay State. Each denomination held firmly to its body of theological beliefs, though it realized these could not be introduced into the public schools. All were naturally united, in good part for self-preservation, in opposing the teaching of the old creed.

Prolonged controversy in the first quarter of the nineteenth century, during which pamphlets, sermons, and open-forum letters flowed from pen and pulpit, at last led to an irreparable break between the Liberals and the orthodox Calvinists, and the founding of the Unitarian Church by the former group. The Congregationalist Church was legally disestablished in 1833. Horace Mann, of course, affiliated himself with the Liberals and the Unitarians.

Throughout his childhood and into his adulthood, Mann was keenly conscious of the atmosphere of sectarian strife by which he was surrounded. His assumption of the Secretaryship of the Board of Education forced him to become personally involved. During his twelve years in that office and later as President of Antioch College, his views on moral and religious education were under almost constant assault. The issue was always the same —the place of religious instruction in the schools—and it lay at the heart of all the controversies in which Mann engaged. From the first day, the eyes of the orthodox were fixed upon him, ready for attack, given the slightest provocation.

Scarcely had the new Secretary taken over his duties when criticism began. The occasion was his first circuit of the school conventions in 1837, when Mann passed the Sabbath in Edgartown. Instead of attending services in one of the town's three orthodox churches, he chose to visit a nearby Indian village, thereby incurring the ill-will of the local clergy. The following year the denominational press began to question the effect of the Board's policies on religious instruction in the schools. In March, 1838, Frederick A. Packard of Philadelphia, Recording Secretary and Editor of Publications of the American Sunday School Union, who (as noted in Chapter 6) was incensed at Mann's refusal to approve inclusion of the Union's publications in the public school libraries, began a series of five letters which appeared in successive issues of the *New York Observer* and the *Boston Recorder*. Earlier, Packard had addressed a meeting of 200 prominent Congregational ministers, charging Mann and the Board with selecting books which were "anti-evangelical," and warning the ministers to be on their guard against the Secretary's antireligious bias. The *Observer* and *Recorder* articles, all anonymous, reiterated the charges and predicted dire consequences for the schools if the Board persisted in its policies.

Dissension on the Board itself soon cropped up. Though the Board's membership was predominantly liberal, it included, as previously noted, an arch-conservative Episcopalian, Edward A. Newton, a strong supporter of the Established Church of England. Newton was essentially unsympathetic to the separation of church and state and to a secular common school system which banned the teaching of religion. Since he was unable to persuade other members of the Board on the matter of the school libraries' contents, his resignation from the Board was tendered to Governor Everett—a departure which Mann thought was good riddance. Several years later, in an unsigned article in the *Christian Witness,* Newton renewed his attack with the charge that Mann's advocacy of nonsectarian religious instruction in the public schools differed in no important respect from Stephen Girard's plan for establishing an orphanage and college in Philadelphia. Girard's will prohibited the teaching of religion in his school and even the presence of clergymen within its buildings.

The persistent criticisms of Mann and the Board by Newton and the orthodox in general may be summed up as follows: exclusion of sectarian teaching in the public schools was subversive of Christianity and morality; the common school library undermined orthodox religion by refusing to admit the writings of Luther, Calvin, Knox, Cranmer, Wesley, and Fuller; the *Common School Journal,* the Secretary's *Reports,* and the normal schools were elements in a system designed to rob the people of their ancient faith; Mann's and the Board's interpretation of the school law of 1827, banning sectarian instruction, was erroneous, for the law was never intended to exclude from the schools the teaching of the great doctrines of the Gospel, but only to exclude the teaching of church government and discipline; the *Shorter Catechism* should be restored and orthodox doctrines of grace should be taught, as a great majority of the people were orthodox; and, finally, the Board itself, "wholly useless and burdensome as a State institution," was usurping power, was antidemocratic, and was constantly violating cherished principles of local government.

Most of the attacks on him and the Board of Education were attributed by Mann to the old-line Calvinists, the orthodox, who had a vested interest in maintaining their hold on the educational system. A characteristic response by Mann was an article in the *Common School Journal,* stating, in part: "Probably they will have no difficulty in making out that the Board is irreligious; for with them religion is synonomous with Calvin's five points. As for St. James's definition of it, 'pure religion and undefiled is to visit the fatherless and widows in their affliction,' &c.; and that other definition, 'Do justly, love mercy, and walk humbly with thy God,'—the Orthodox have quite outgrown these obsolete notions, and have got a religion which can at once gratify their self-esteem and destructiveness. They shall not unclinch me from my labors for mankind." On another occasion, Mann wrote, "The Orthodox have hunted me this winter as though they were bloodhounds, and I a poor rabbit."

Three letters were published by Mann in refutation of the charge that he was attempting to establish a godless system of public schools; therein he stated forcefully, clearly, and with considerable heat the principles which he understood to be involved in the dispute, and corrected misstatements and misrepresentations. It was noted that the law of 1827 specifically barred sectarian teaching from the schools, and then a query was posed: "Is the exclusion of sectarianism synonymous with the exclusion of Christianity?" Actually, Mann maintained, the Board had been responsible for a great increase in Bible reading in the schools. The Board had formal jurisdiction only in the normal schools, where the Bible was required to be read each day. Christian teaching without sectarian bias was encouraged and several of the books approved by the Board "breathe the purest sentiments of Christianity, and glow with the spirit of devotion; while not a single work of an opposite character or tendency has been admitted into the series."

In one of his letters, Mann lists the principles of Christian faith which he felt could be taught to children in the common schools without violating the constitutional provision against teaching sectarianism:

"1. To love the Lord their God with all their heart, and their
   neighbor as themselves;
 2. To do to others as they would be done by;
 3. To do justly, to love mercy and to walk humbly with God;
 4. To visit the fatherless and widows in their affliction and to
   keep themselves unspotted from the world;
 5. To honor father and mother;
 6. To keep the Sabbath holy;
 7. Not to steal;
 8. Not to kill;
 9. Not to bear false witness against neighbors;
10. Not to covet."[46]

Mann's first letter appeared in the *Christian Witness,* official
organ of the Massachusetts Episcopal diocese, edited by M. A.
DeWolfe Howe, who replied to Mann's list of specific truths of
Christianity by conceding: "They are very well so far as they go;
they are important to the social uprightness and welfare of man,
but they leave untouched what we, and all Orthodox Christians
esteem the essentials of Christianity,—the way of salvation by
Jesus Christ." To Mann's claim that the Board was responsible for
an increase in religious teaching, Howe declared, "More teachers
impart something which *they* call religion. But some are silenced,
or modified into moral lecturers, who once dispensed truths
which *are* religion." Howe refused to print Mann's second and
third letters, which appeared in the Boston *Daily Courier.*
   In reality, as Mann pointed out in one of his letters, there had
been a steady trend away from sectarian instruction in the public
schools prior to the establishment of the Board of Education:

In nine eastern counties of the State, containing more than five eighths
of its population, the teaching of the Assembly's Catechism and of
Orthodox doctrines, had been, not entirely, but mainly discontinued,
long before the existence of the Board. The Catechism had been objected to by the Orthodox Baptists themselves. In many places, the
discontinuance dates back, at least, to the beginning of the present
century. I have met with many persons, educated in our schools, who
never saw the Assembly's Catechism. So convinced was public sentiment
of the equity and justice of the law of 1827, against sectarian teaching in
the schools, that in all the common school conventions I have ever

attended, in almost all of which the subject of moral and religious instruction had been introduced, there has been but one instance where such teaching was advocated; and there it was resisted on the spot by an Orthodox clergyman.

Mann added that in the more than one thousand school committee reports received in his office, all except two were averse to sectarian teaching in the schools. He goes on to demolish a statement by Newton—that nine-tenths of the Commonwealth's population belong to orthodox denominations—by citing figures for the membership of other groups: Universalists, Unitarians, Catholics, etc. Patently, what the conservative churchmen desired was to restore their own particular brand of sectarianism to the schools; Horace Mann, on the other hand, knew that in schools serving the entire Commonwealth, containing various sects, such a scheme was neither practicable nor desirable.

A renewal of the controversy was triggered by Mann's *Seventh Annual Report,* in which he had criticized the English system of church-controlled education, a system which resulted in neglect of the common schools and widespread illiteracy. Mann's purpose in calling attention to the miserable state of the English schools, he explained, was as "an antidote against attempting the same things here." In the eyes of the ultra-orthodox of Massachusetts, however, Mann's censure of the English schools was interpreted as an attack on the Established Church. Such individuals as Newton took strong exception to an article by Mann in the *Common School Journal* in which he asserted: "The only reason why there has not, long ago, been a system of public instruction in England is, because the church steadfastly resists all legal provisions for literary and moral education unless it can control it for the purpose of proselytism."

The dispute simmered for a time until another outburst in 1846, initiated by the Reverend Matthew Hale Smith. In a sermon preached before the Church and the Society of the Pilgrims in Boston, the orthodox minister held forth upon the "Increase of Intemperance: Crime and Juvenile Depravity—It Cause and Cure." Immorality and crime, it was charged, were increasing at a rapid rate because of the absence of good home training and attempts to amend the legislation of God. Modern reformers had assumed responsibility for the education of youth and in the process had abandoned divinely appointed agencies for repressing crime and cultivating virtue. "Men, wise above that which is written," declared Smith, "have made common schools the theatre of their experiments and labors." The public schools of Boston were denounced as corrupt and corrupting, after which Smith turned his guns on the Board of Education:

An effort has been made, and that too with some success, to do three things with our common schools: (1) To get out of them the Bible and all religious instruction; (2) to abolish the use of the rod and all correction but a little talk; (3) to make common schools a counterpoise to religious instruction at home and in Sabbath schools. The Board of Education in Massachusetts has aided in this work in two ways: (1) By allowing an individual, under the sanction of its authority, to disseminate through the land crude and destructive principles, principles believed to be at war with the Bible and with the best interests of the young for time and eternity. (2) By a library which excludes books as sectarian that inculcate truths which nine-tenths of professed Christians of all names believe, while it accepts others that inculcate the most deadly heresy—even universal salvation.[47]

Mann felt compelled to respond to the Reverend Smith's broadside, aimed at him and the Board. The principal points of his rejoinder were: first, the primary responsibility for Bible or moral instruction was in the hands of local school committees, over whom the Board had no authority; second, "The whole influence of the Board of Education, from the day of its organization to the present time, has been to promote and encourage, and whenever they have had any power, as in the case of the Normal schools, to direct the daily use of the Bible in schools"; third, the Board had never attempted to abolish the use of the rod in schools and accepted corporal punishment when other means of restraint had been tried and failed, but it steadfastly opposed the enormous abuses of the rod perpetrated by incompetent teachers; fourth, the Common School Library books were selected with the most meticulous care, and none had been accepted until they had been unanimously approved by the orthodox and liberal members of the Board alike.

Reviewing the prolonged controversies with Packard, Newton,

Smith, Howe, and their like, a recent Mann biographer, Jonathan Messerli, asks: "Why did Mann expend so much of his limited time and energy on such small fry? Somehow," Messerli concludes, "he could never emancipate his mind from a conspiracy and persecution complex when even the slightest opposition to him appeared in print," despite the fact that he had almost complete support from the press and from what Mann himself referred to as "the best portion of the orthodox," "almost all the other denominations," and "even the great mass of the Episcopalians themselves."[48]

Certain central ideas constitute Horace Mann's philosophy of moral and religious education—themes which recur over and over again in the *Annual Reports,* in speeches on education and religion, and in articles in the *Common School Journal.* No fair-minded person can accuse him of lacking spirituality after reading his views. Neil Gerald McCluskey, in his *Public Schools and Moral Education,* summarizes the predominant Mann theses as follows:

1. The principal aim of education is the development of the child's moral and religious character. There should be no attempt to separate morality and religion, i.e., the "nonsectarian" or "natural" religion.

2. Character formation is the direct responsibility of the common school; in fact, the common school is the most perfect agency for such formation.

3. As much religious instruction must be given in the common school as is compatible with religious freedom. In teaching religion the school must not favor any one sect in the community but should inculcate the generally agreed upon moral and religious beliefs of Christianity. The sectarian spirit is by every means to be shunned.

4. Natural religion (i.e., the "religion of heaven" as opposed to man-made creedal religions) means obedience to all of God's laws—physical, moral, spiritual, religious. This is the true substance of Christianity, whose primary law is the Golden Rule.

5. The Bible, without note or interpreter, is the means par excellence of realizing this primary aim of education because it breathes God's laws and presents illustrious examples of conduct, above all that of Jesus Christ.[49]

Mann has frequently been described as an evangelist for the public schools, and some of his statements on education undoubtedly have the flavor of sermons. Note, for example, the evangelical fervor of these comments on the Massachusetts public school system at the conclusion of his twelve years as Secretary: "In a social and political sense, it is a *free* school system. It knows no distinction of rich and poor, of bond or free, or between those, who, in the imperfect light of this world, are seeking, through different channels, to reach the gate of heaven. Without money and without price, it throws open its doors, and spreads the table of its bounty, for all the children of the state. Like the sun, it shines not only upon the good, but upon the evil, that they may become good; and, like the rain, its blessings descend not only upon the just, but upon the unjust, that their injustice may depart from them, and be known no more."[50]

To Horace Mann, the essence of religion was love for humanity, the Golden Rule, and the social betterment of the race. In matters of religion, all human authority was suspect.

Eventually, the religious controversies died away, in good part because Mann had a solid majority of the people on his side. The main issue had been firmly settled, i.e., that in Massachusetts "no one sect shall obtain any advantage over other sects by means of the school, which, for purposes of self-preservation, it has established."

In his final report as Secretary, Mann again quotes with approval, as he had on numerous occasions, the 1827 law directing all teachers to instill "the principles of piety, justice and a sacred regard to truth, love to their country, humanity and universal benevolence, sobriety, industry, and frugality, chastity, moderation, and temperance, and those other virtues which are the ornament of human society, and the basis upon which a republican constitution is founded." "Are not these virtues and graces part and parcel of Christianity?" Mann asks. "In other words, can there be Christianity without them? While these virtues and these duties towards God and man, are inculcated in our schools, any one who says that the schools are anti-Christian or un-Christian, expressly affirms that his own system of Christianity does not embrace any one of this radiant catalogue; that it rejects them all; that it embraces their opposites!"[51]

CHAPTER 9

European Pilgrimage

A deep interest in European educational methods and systems among Americans predated Horace Mann's appointment to the Secretaryship of the Board of Education. Following visits abroad, Alexander D. Bache, professor of physics and president of Girard College in Philadelphia, and Calvin E. Stowe, Ohio educator, had published widely read reports, based on tours abroad; Victor Cousin, French minister of instruction, had produced a report on education in Prussia, which was translated into English and had many American readers; Americans attending German universities had observed and reported on education in the German states; and Bronson Alcott had introduced Pestalozzian ideas to a group of Massachusetts teachers. Nevertheless, it does not appear that up to Mann's time American educational thought had been more than superficially influenced by foreign practices or concepts.

In an introduction to the Board of Education's *Seventh Annual Report,* Governor Briggs noted that "The Secretary of the Board having impaired his health by a laborious and unremitting attention to the duties of his office, and having proposed to the Board to visit, at his own expense, several countries of Europe, as well for the restoration of his health as for the opportunity of more extensive observation of the means of education, the Board very willingly accepted the proposition, fraught as they believed, with great advantages to the cause of common school education in this country."[52]

Mann himself pointed out that for the past six years he had

applied himself most assiduously to the responsibilities of the Secretaryship, had visited schools in most of the "Free States" and in several of the "Slave States," had attended great numbers of educational meetings, and otherwise had conscientiously fulfilled his duties. Yet "the celebrity of institutions in foreign countries" had attracted his attention, filling him with "an intense desire of knowing whether, in any respect, those institutions were superior to our own; and, if anything were found in them worthy of adoption, of transferring it for our improvement." Further, Mann stressed that "the severe and unmitigating labor" which he had been called on to perform as Secretary had seriously impaired his health. To forestall possible criticism by his enemies, however, he stated that the visit was to be made *"at my own expense"* (Mann's italics).

On the day of his departure, May 1, 1843, Mann was married to Mary Peabody, Nathaniel Hawthorne's sister-in-law. Mann's friends urged him to make his European tour a real vacation and a true honeymoon, but he considered that he had been given leave of absence to study educational systems abroad and nothing could persuade him to deviate from his chief mission. Consequently, the six-month sabbatical was more educational than recreational. So completely engrossed was Mann in his educational investigations that he had little time for or patience with ordinary sightseeing.

Of first importance to Mann was to find "beacons to terrify as well as lights to guide" the American people in their educational and social advance. Every day was scheduled to the hilt, from seven in the morning until five in the afternoon, for visiting various types of institutions and conferring with leaders in education and social reform. Many of the free evenings were spent reading descriptive documents which Mann hoped would improve his understanding of what he was seeing.

The Manns' travels took them to England, Ireland, and Scotland, after which they "crossed the German Ocean to Hamburgh, thence went to Magdeburgh, Berlin, Potsdam, Halle and Weissenfels, in the Kingdom of Prussia; to Leipsic and Dresden, the two great cities in the Kingdom of Saxony; thence to Erfurt, Weimar, Eisenach, etc., on the great route from the middle of Germany to Frankfort on the Maine; thence to the Grand Duchy of Nassau, of Hesse Darmstadt and of Baden, and after visiting all the principal cities in the Rhenish Provinces of Prussia, passed through Holland and Belgium to Paris."

Mann's interests were far too broad to be limited to the common schools. Schools, schoolhouses, school systems, apparatus, and teaching methods were first on his agenda. At every opportunity, therefore, he visited elementary schools, public and private; all normal schools; schools for teaching the handicapped, such as the blind and the deaf; schools for the reformation of juvenile offenders; all charity foundations for educating the children of the poor and of criminals; and all orphan establishments. Secondary schools, colleges, and universities were also on his itinerary. In addition to educational institutions, Mann reported that he "visited great numbers of hospitals for the insane, and for the sick, and also of prisons. This I have done not only from a rational curiosity to know in what manner these classes of our fellow beings are treated abroad; but in the hope of finding something by which we might be enlightened and improved in the management of the same classes at home." Mann's experience as a member of the managing board of the Worcester Hospital for the Insane had given him a vital interest in Seguin's schools for idiots. Abroad, he saw no insane asylums he considered superior to, or even equal to, the Worcester institution; and the prisons, especially on the Continent, were "almost uniformly in a most deplorable condition."

Mann was deeply disappointed in the general condition of British schools. The glaring contrasts between social classes struck him forcibly and painfully. In London, the Manns lived near Regent's Park and there they saw "such splendid mansions and equipages and such squalid misery side by side." Mann was profoundly touched by the plight of London's children of the poor, an innumerable lot of whom had served terms in prison by the age of twelve. In his view, Great Britain had a magnificent façade but was "tortured in all its vitals by the pangs of want and deadly wounds" due to its poor schools and the exploitation of the lower orders by the manufacturers. The wealthier classes, naturally a small minority of the population, maintained excellent schools for their own children, while being unconcerned with providing educational opportunities for the great majority, the neglected poorer classes, or even actively opposed the support of public schools. The private school teachers, too, fought vigorously against any threat to their vested interests. Mann, with his abiding faith in democracy, was offended by any system of education or society in which the underdog was denied an equal opportunity. His belief was that neither education nor democracy can exist without the other.

Mann found much more to commend about the Scottish schools. The teaching methods impressed him and the liveliness of the classrooms amazed him. All teachers were college graduates or had attended universities before beginning their careers. Most admirable, Mann thought, was

the mental activity with which the exercises were conducted, both on the part of teachers and pupils. . . .I do not exaggerate when I say that the most active and lively schools I have ever seen in the United States, must be regarded almost as dormitories, if compared with the fervid life of the Scotch schools; and, by the side of theirs, our pupils would seem to be hybernating animals just emerging from their torpid state, and as yet but half conscious of the possession of life and faculties. It is certainly within bounds to say, that there were six times as many questions put and answers given, in the same space of time, as I ever heard put and given in any school in our own country.[53]

In keeping with the intense mental activity, the teacher was in constant motion—"I never saw a teacher in Scotland sitting in a schoolroom." Further, "nor are the bodies of the pupils mere blocks, resting motionless in their seats, or lolling from side to side as though life were deserting them. The custom is for each pupil to rise when giving an answer . . . the scene becomes full of animation when a dozen or twenty at once spring to their feet and ejaculate at the top of their voices." Those who answered correctly were moved to the head of the class. "I have seen a school kept for two hours in succession, in this state of intense mental activity," observed Mann, "with nothing more than an alternation of subjects during the time, or perhaps the relaxation of singing." One feature of the Scottish schools, on the other hand, disturbed Mann. Prizes were given to the best students and the children were thereby placed under too great strain. The aim, in Mann's view, should be for each pupil to be ambitious to outdo himself, not his classmates.

From the outset, Horace Mann's principal destination was Germany, then the center of the teacher-training movement, and doubtless having the best common school system in the world. Educators were going to Germany in great numbers for inspiration and information and then returning to their homelands to introduce the Prussian system. From Hull the Manns crossed the North Sea and spent more than two months visiting German schools in Hamburg, Berlin, Potsdam, Halle, Weissenfels, Leipzig, Dresden, Erfurt, Weimar, Eisenach, Frankfurt, Baden, and the principal cities of the Rhenish provinces. The questions for which Mann sought answers concerning the German schools were these: "What branches are taught in them? What are the modes and processes of teaching? What incitements or motive-powers are employed, for stimulating the pupils to learn? In fine, what is done when teacher and pupils meet each other face to face in the schoolroom, how is it done, and with what success?"

Mann begins his report on the German educational system with a number of general observations, discussed in some detail. He notes the extensive authority and control assumed by government agencies over the youth of the state, though primarily, he thinks, for the welfare of the children. He was next struck by "the number and populousness of their orphan establishments," mainly filled by the children of soldiers who had died in Europe's wars. In the Royal Orphan House at Potsdam, for instance, there were a thousand boys—all sons of soldiers. Two other types of institution admired by Mann were schools established in connection with prisons, to educate the children of criminals, and re-formatory institutions for youthful offenders—all efficiently and humanely administered, not for purposes of punishment, but for salvaging the young for society.

An important element in the superiority of Prussian schools, in Mann's estimation, was the proper classification of students. "In all places where the numbers are sufficiently large to allow it," he states, "the children are divided according to ages and attainments; and a single teacher has the charge only of a single class, or of as small a number of classes as is practicable."

Methods of teaching young children in German schools was a subject of keen interest to Mann and he dwelt upon the matter at length under various headings: instruction in reading; arithmetic and mathematics; grammar and composition; writing and drawing; geography; nature study; Bible history and knowledge; and music. "About twenty years ago," Mann comments, "teachers in Prussia made the important discovery that children have five senses,—together with various muscles and mental faculties,—all which, almost by a necessity of their nature, must be kept in a state of activity, and which, if not usefully, are liable to be mischievously employed." The art of teaching, therefore, is most effective if all senses, muscles, and faculties are fully utilized.

Mann found admirable, for example, the German techniques for teaching reading, which began with the word method instead of the alphabet. In one class which he visited and described, "there were elements of reading, spelling, writing, grammar and drawing, interspersed with anecdotes and not a little general information" successfully combined. A vivid picture of the techniques employed is presented in Mann's description:

The Prussian teachers, by their constant habit of conversing with the pupils; by requiring a complete answer to be given to every question; by never allowing a mistake in termination or in the collocation of words or clauses to pass uncorrected, nor the sentence as corrected to pass unrepeated; by requiring the poetry of the reading lessons to be changed into oral, or written prose, and the prose to be paraphrased, or expressed in different words; and by exacting a general account or summary of the reading lessons, are constantly teaching grammar or the German language.[54]

Equally imaginative and effective methods were utilized for the teaching of writing and drawing, geography, arithmetic, music, and other subjects in all the schools seen by Mann, in country or city, for the children of the rich or for the poor, including "schools connected with pauper establishments, with houses of correction or with prisons."

After six weeks spent in visiting schools in Prussia and Saxony, Mann was most impressed by three facts:

(1) During all this time, I never saw a teacher hearing a lesson of any kind,

(excepting a reading or spelling lesson,) *with a book in his hand;* (2) I never saw a teacher *sitting,* while hearing a recitation; (3) Though I saw hundreds of schools, and . . . tens of thousands of pupils, *I never saw one child undergoing punishment, or arraigned for misconduct. I never saw one child in tears from having been punished, or from fear of being punished.* [55]

The teachers were so thoroughly grounded in their subjects, with "their libraries in their heads," that it was unnecessary for them to carry books to their classes. While recitations were being heard, teachers mingled with their pupils, "passing rapidly from one side of the class to the other, animating, encouraging, sympathizing, breathing life into less active natures, assuring the timid, distributing encouragement and endearment to all." Here Mann drew an analogy from his courtroom experience. A good lawyer would never dream of planting himself lazily in a chair, reading from some old book which the jury could hardly understand, and after droning away for an hour leave the court; if he did, he would lose "not only his own reputation, but the cause of his client also."

On the question of discipline, a matter which was later to involve Mann in heated controversy, Mann commented at length on "the beautiful relation of harmony and affection" between teacher and pupil. "During all the time mentioned," he declares, "I never saw a blow struck, I never heard a sharp rebuke given, I never saw a child in tears, nor arraigned at the teacher's bar for any alleged misconduct. . . . I heard no child ridiculed, sneered at, or scolded, for making a mistake. . . . On the contrary, the relation seemed to be one of duty first, and then affection, on the part of the teachers,—of affection first, and then duty, on the part of the scholar." [56]

The high level of teaching in the German schools was attributed by Mann in considerable measure to the seminaries for teachers. Students spent three years in residence at these institutions, during which misfits were weeded out rigorously. Students were selected with care and individuals who had failed in other professions or businesses had little chance for admission to "this sacred calling." The end result, Mann concludes, was to produce a body of men with "more benevolence and self-sacrifice than the legal or medical professions, while they have less of sanctimoniousness and austerity, less of indisposition to enter into all the innocent amusements and joyous feelings of childhood than the clerical." Elsewhere in his travels, in Scotland, Ireland, and France, Mann commended the existing normal schools, too, for their wholesome effect in upgrading the teaching profession.

Other features of the Prussian school system attracted Mann's attention. A corps of school inspectors, "selected from among the most talented and educated men in the community," he believed were instrumental in "bringing up teachers to a high standard of qualifications, at the beginning; and in creating, at last, a self-motive, self-improving spirit among them." Also of prime importance was "the universality of the children's attendance" at school, a decided contrast to the situation in Mann's home state of Massachusetts. In Prussian schools, "the only two *absolute* grounds of exemption from attendance, are sickness and death." Parents who failed to comply with the law were severely punished.

At the conclusion of his review of the German educational system, Mann attempts to answer a broader question, one affecting the entire society: "Why with such a wide-extended and energetic machinery for public instruction, the Prussians, as a people, do not rise more rapidly in the scale of civilization; why the mechanical and useful arts remain among them in such a half-barbarous condition; why the people are so sluggish and unenterprising in their character; and finally, why certain national vices are not yet extirpated."[57]

Among the reasons why the educational system had failed to solve the nation's problems, in Mann's view, were these: the children were withdrawn from school at too early an age, namely, fourteen, and their progress thereby suddenly arrested; there was "a great dearth of suitable books for the reading of the older children or younger men"; when the children left school, society made "little use either of the faculties that have been developed, or of the knowledge that has been acquired," chiefly because of an autocratic government, in which citizens had no opportunity for democratic participation; and, finally, as to the Prussians' vices, "they are the vices of the sovereign and of the higher classes of society, copied by the lower, without the decorations which gilded them in their upper sphere."

Near the conclusion of his report, Mann reviews his findings on the use of corporal punishment in the schools of countries other than Prussia. He noted that such punishment was obsolete in Holland, in fact was illegal, though occasionally hopelessly incorrigible students, guilty of chronic bad conduct, were expelled. In the Scottish schools, misconduct and poor recitations in class were subject to blows by the teacher, leading Mann to state: "Could the Scotch teacher add something more of gentleness to his prodigious energy and vivacity, and were the general influences which he imparts to his pupils, modified in one or two particulars, he would become a model teacher for the world." In England, a variety of practices were found, ranging from schools in which "talent and accomplishment have wholly superseded corporal punishment" to others in which the teacher maintained his control by vicious punishment of children guilty of even minor infractions. The practice in Paris schools was to exert strict surveillance over the behavior of students, "to supersede the necessity of punishment by taking away all opportunity for transgression."

Summing up, Mann suggests "At all times and in all countries, the rule is the same;—the punishment of scholars [students] is the *complement* of the proper treatment of children by parents at home, and the competency of the teacher in school."

Because the issue was so highly sensitive at home, Horace Mann made particular inquiries about moral and religious instruction in schools abroad, "to learn in what manner and to what extent, moral and religious instruction is given in schools." Here again, there was extensive variation in practices. For example, it was found that "Nothing receives more attention in the Prussian schools than the Bible. It is taken up early and studied systematically." Sectarianism was also taught in all Prussian schools: Luther's Catechism in the Protestant schools and the Catholic Catechism in the Roman Catholic schools. A considerable number of the teachers were "inwardly hostile to the doctrines they are required to teach." Concluding his survey, Mann observes: "To a vast extent, abroad, I found religion to be used for political purposes;—not to enthrone a Deity in the heavens, but a king over a state;—not to secure the spontaneous performance of good works to men, but the blind submission of person and

property to the ruler." More than ever, therefore, he was convinced of the rightness of separating church and state and the
banning of sectarian teaching in public schools.

By the time the Manns reached Holland they were suffering
from fatigue and homesickness. Relatively scant attention, accordingly, is paid to the schools of that country, and to those of
France, the final stop. France was the country where normal
schools originated and from which they derived their name,
giving Mann a special reason to visit Paris. Several schools in and
around Paris were inspected, but Mann was disappointed to
discover that instruction seemed stereotyped, and students were
trained in memory alone, with little opportunity for original
thinking. He considered it worthy of mention, however, "as one
of the proofs of the advancement, (however slow,) of the race,
that the Normal School now in successful operation at Versailles,
occupies the very site,—some of its buildings are the very buildings, and its beautiful grounds the very grounds,—which were
the dog-kennels of Louis XIV, and his royal successors."

In ranking the educational systems of Europe which he had the
opportunity to visit, Mann had no hesitation in placing Prussia
first, followed in order by Saxony, the western and southwestern
states of Germany, Holland and Scotland, Ireland, France, Belgium, and England. Prussia was decidedly the best of them all;
gradual deterioration of the schools occurred as the Rhine was
approached, and they were decidedly inferior in Nassau, Hesse,
Darmstadt, and Baden, and the cities of Cologne, Coblentz, and
Dusseldorf. England was found to be poorest of all.

Looking back upon his five-month tour, Mann found much to
admire and considerable to condemn. Some states had strong
national educational systems, carefully regulated; others had
scarcely a semblance of an organization. Some teachers enriched
their instruction with explanation and illustration, while others
demanded sheer verbal memory. Corporal punishment was used
to excess in some countries, banned in others. Ireland suffered
under the double handicaps of Catholicism and English persecution; the Scots had remarkable influence over pupils, but were too
attached to "a wholly formal knowledge and an arbitrary application of the passages of the Bible"; Germany was split between two
principal confessions, with danger of inconsistency and skepti-

cism; and education in Italy and the Mediterranean countries, from what Mann could learn of it, was so deficient that "no father would want his child to grow up there."

In certain respects, Mann decided that Massachusetts schools were superior to the European; in others, the opposite was true. In any event, by the time of his return home he had seen what he went to see and was ready to apply his newly acquired knowledge to the Massachusetts scene.

CHAPTER 10

The Boston Schoolmasters' Controversy

Horace Mann returned from his European travels fatigued but in a state of euphoria. A review of the *Seventh Annual Report* in the London *Athenaeum,* usually anti-American, was complimentary, the German and English governments reprinted the report for distribution in their own countries, and commendatory letters were received from correspondents in England, Scotland, Italy, and elsewhere.

Opposition, however, was building up. In a letter to George Combe in April, 1844, Mann wrote, "My report, generally speaking, has met with unusual favor, but there are owls who, to adapt the world to their own eyesight, would always keep the sun from shining. Most teachers amongst us have been animated to greater exertions by the account of the best schools abroad. Others are offended at being driven out of the paradise which their own self-esteem had erected for them."

Mann's outspoken criticism of the Massachusetts school system had aroused resentment among those who were the targets for his comments. They could not easily forgive or forget such phrases as "incompetent teachers," "ignorance of teachers," "depressed state of common schools," "sleepy supervision," deficiencies of teachers in the "two indispensable prerequisites for their office," and a charge that the schools had "fallen into a state of general unsoundness and debility."

Opposition to Mann among teachers, somewhat dormant prior

to his mission abroad, became lively and open with the publication of the *Seventh Annual Report.* Mann had foreseen that his praise of Prussian pedagogy would be received as an indirect slap at Massachusetts methods. It was doubtless for this reason that his laudatory comments on "the beautiful relation of harmony and affection which subsisted between teacher and pupils" and the absence of corporal punishment in the German schools was followed by an explanatory statement:

I mean no disparagement of our own teachers by the remark I am about to make. As a general fact, these teachers are as good as public opinion has demanded; as good as the public sentiment has been disposed to appreciate; as good as public liberality has been ready to reward; as good as the preliminary measures taken to qualify them would authorize us to expect. But it was impossible to put down the questionings of my own mind,—whether a visitor could spend six weeks in our own schools without ever hearing an angry word spoken, or seeing a blow struck, or witnessing the flow of tears.[58]

This was the spark that ignited the flame. Though Mann had phrased the situation as diplomatically as possible, the Massachusetts schoolmasters recognized at once that they had been damned with faint praise and reacted accordingly. Shortly there appeared a lengthy pamphlet of 144 pages, entitled *Remarks on the Seventh Annual Report of the Hon. Horace Mann, Secretary of the Massachusetts Board of Education* (Boston, 1844), prepared and signed by thirty-one Boston schoolmasters. The *Remarks* were intended, it was stated, "in some degree to correct erroneous views and impressions, and thus tend to promote a healthy tone in public sentiment in relation to many things connected with the welfare of our common schools." Each of the four divisions came from a different pen. First was a eulogy for the schools as they had been founded and preserved from the days of the Pilgrim Fathers; they were *"never more prosperous than at the time the Board of Education was formed."* Improvement in the common schools was desirable, the schoolmasters agreed, but not *revolution,* as advocated by the Secretary. Exaggerated claims, they asserted, were being made by the normal schools in the preparation of teachers; further, their heads lacked practical experience in public school teaching, and, in any case, subject matter far transcended methodology in importance. Mann was charged with being out of sympathy with the public school teachers and had condemned and disparaged their work, though "It is not known that he had ever given much attention to the common school system, or that he had been in any way very active in the great cause of common schools, before his appointment as Secretary of the Board."

The second section of the schoolmasters' assault discussed the Prussian schools. Looking at the matter as "practical educators," the masters concluded that Mann had spent insufficient time in Prussia to be competent to judge the system objectively and to evaluate teaching practices. About some features he was overenthusiastic, while failing to recognize weaknesses. Oral teaching stimulated student interest while neglecting the formation of "the habit of independent and individual effort." Mann had objected to overreliance on textbooks; the schoolmasters defended them as essential instruments of education. Part 2 closed by denouncing Mann, in effect, as an academic and moral amateur unqualified to criticize experienced teachers, and condemning "those *imaginative* educators, who would substitute the pleasing fictions of speculation, for the sound and sober dictates of reason."

Section 3 of the schoolmasters' document hit at Mann on another front—for his support of the word method of learning to read. The masters' objections to the theory were set forth in what Mann's biographer, E. I. F. Williams, correctly describes as "labored and often specious reasoning." The masters viewed with alarm Mann's "pleasure promoting principle" in the relationship of pupil and teacher, "that of affection first, and then duty." The Boston schoolmasters, with strong Puritan traditions in their heredity and background, insisted that "duty should come first, and pleasure should grow out of the discharge of it."

The hottest issue of all was raised in the fourth and final section of the schoolmasters' philippic, the question of school discipline and corporal punishment. To comprehend the teachers' point of view, one needs to recall traditions dating back to the colonial era. Even at Harvard it had been the custom for the president to inflict corporal punishment upon unruly students. Incompetent teachers found the switch to be the easiest instrument with which to control children. To Mann, "The power of inflicting bodily pain is the lowest form of superiority. It is the instinctive resort of brute animals, which, having no resources in intelligence, appeal to force. It prevails most universally amongst the most savage tribes, whose superiority of muscular power gives superiority of social rank, and the regal title is conceded to the strongest." Corporal punishment's effect on children was traumatic, Mann believed, because it relied upon the debasing emotion of fear. "You cannot open blossoms with a storm but under the genial influences of the sun," he declared, adding "The very blows which beat arithmetic and grammar in, beat confidence and manliness out. They lead to hatred, fraud, lying, revenge." His observations abroad strengthened Mann's convictions against corporal punishment.

Mann did not go so far, however, as to maintain that the rod should never be used: "I would by no means be understood to express the opinion that, *in the present state of society,* punishment, and even corporal punishment can be dispensed with, by all teachers, in all schools, and with regard to all scholars. Order is emphatically the first law of a schoolroom." Mann added, "This, however, is certain, that when a teacher preserves order and secures progress, the minimum of punishment shows the maximum of qualifications."[59]

Well in advance of Mann's appointment as Secretary of the Board of Education, public attitudes toward corporal punishment had begun to change, though there were still sharp divergencies of opinion. Thomas Jefferson had declared himself against the practice. In 1838, Henry Barnard, in a lecture before the primary teachers of Boston, had offended some of his audience by urging curtailment of corporal punishment, and a short time later a petition had been presented to the school committee of Boston urging discontinuance of corporal punishment for girls. The petition was disapproved, but a resolution passed "to strictly enjoin upon the several instructors of the public schools never to make use of corporal punishment until every other means of influencing the pupil shall have failed." Henceforth, to prevent abuses, it was ruled that a record should be maintained of all cases of corporal punishments and, if necessary for them to be inflicted, they were to be administered in the presence of all teachers in the school.

The response of the Boston schoolmasters (now banded together as the Principals' Association) to the pro and con arguments was strictly authoritarian. "All school order," they declared, "like that of the family and society, must be established upon the basis of acknowledged authority, as a starting point." The teacher has both the right and the duty to establish and enforce such authority "by an appeal to the most appropriate motives that a true heart and sound mind may select among all those which God had implanted in our nature." High are preferable to low motives, but any are acceptable "which circumstances may render fitting, . . . even the fear of physical pain; for we believe that that, low as it is, will have its place, its proper sphere of influence, not for a limited period merely, till teachers can become better qualified and society more morally refined, but while men and children continue to be human; that is, so long as schools and schoolmasters and governments and laws are needed."

A person of Mann's disposition could hardly have been expected to submit meekly to the schoolmasters' *Remarks*. In his view, the masters had carefully selected certain of his statements, twisted them out of context, and drawn conclusions opposite in sense to those intended. About two months after the *Remarks* appeared, Mann was ready with a furious *Reply to the "Remarks" of Thirty-one Boston Schoolmasters on the Seventh Annual Report of the Secretary of the Massachusetts Board of Education* (Boston, 1844), a document of 176 pages. One Mann biographer, George Allen Hubbell, described the *Reply* as "a poor piece of work . . . until now Mann's writings had been dignified, worthy and strong; but this was written in a bitter and sarcastic spirit, and was hasty and ill-thought-out, and though done with a peculiar strength, he descended to levels in his defense and counterattack quite unworthy of a man of his quality and power." A contemporary critic, Francis Bowen, writing for the *North American Review* in 1845, reacted differently, concluding that the Secretary had not only vindicated himself, but had retaliated upon his attackers with extreme severity; though Mann disliked the use of the rod on children, Bowen went on, he was evidently willing to whip schoolmasters.

In the *Reply* Mann reviews one by one the schoolmen's wide-ranging criticisms. He defends his policy of trying to obtain uniformity in textbooks and restates the Board of Education's policy against showing favor or disfavor to any religion or political party. To the charge that the Board was attempting to eliminate the Bible from the schools, Mann retorts: "The Bible should continue to be used in our schools; but still, that it shall be left with the local authorities,—where the law now leaves it,—to say, in what manner, in what classes, etc., it shall be used." Any sectarian interpretation of the Scriptures in the public school curriculum, however, should not be tolerated.

Near the close of the *Reply,* the Secretary summarizes the trials and tribulations to which he had been subjected since assuming office. The opinion was almost unanimous among enlightened citizens, he thought, that improvements in the common schools were needed, but ideas as to how the improvements were to be effected were frequently opposite and irreconcilable. The cost of providing better schools aroused opposition among many taxpayers. Reductions in the number of textbooks in use had brought down upon the Secretary's head the wrath of book compilers, copyright owners, publishers, and book agents, whose sales had dropped. A highly regarded innovation, the school district libraries, had still provoked objections because of their cost and the nature of the books chosen. The raising of standards for the common schools had thrown many old teachers out of jobs. Private schools, too, had been diminished in number and importance by the upgrading of public schools, creating resentment on that front. Politics and religion were other disturbing elements.

Mann closes the *Reply* with an eloquent appeal to all men to unite in an educational awakening most urgently demanded by the needs of society.

Nothing daunted by the chastisement received from Mann's hands, the schoolmasters appointed a committee to react to the *Reply,* and the following year there came from the press a *Rejoinder to the "Reply" of the Hon. Horace Mann, Secretary of the Massachusetts Board of Education, to the "Remarks" of the Association of Boston Masters Upon his Seventh Annual Report* (Boston, 1845). Two of the masters disassociated themselves from further controversy, leaving twenty-nine to subscribe to the *Rejoinder.* Like their initial work, the *Rejoinder* was divided into four parts, written by different individuals. The author of a section on school discipline, Joseph Hale, was an advocate of the "New Light" Calvinism, an extreme branch of the old orthodox Puritanism, who stoutly defended the practice of corporal punishment in the schools. It was conceded that moral persuasion might be useful in teaching a sense of duty, but Hale insisted upon "the naked doctrine, that physical coercion is, in certain cases, necessary, natural and proper"; he ridiculed the "pseudo-philanthropy" which had made sympathy an abnormal and "predominant feature of the age." In general, the *Rejoinder* simply restated the views presented in the *Remarks,* though in a less offensive manner and tone.

In the same year, Mann came out with his *Answer to the "Rejoinder" of Twenty-nine Boston Schoolmasters, Part of the "Thirty-one" who Published "Remarks" on the Seventh Annual Report of the Secretary of the Massachusetts Board of Education* (Boston, 1845). In this pamphlet of 124 pages, Mann began by tracing the history of the controversy. When he had learned that some of the Boston teachers had found the *Seventh Annual Report* objectionable, he had sought a meeting with them to avoid an open break. After publication of his *Reply* another attempt at peace had been offered. In both instances, his overtures had been rejected and he had no alternative except to defend himself, his friends, his office, and the Board of Education. To erase any doubt among educators and the general public, Mann summed up his code in respect to discipline:

First, that it is the duty of the State to adopt measures for qualifying teachers. Second, that school committeemen are sentinels stationed at the door of every schoolhouse to see that none but the very best teachers who can possibly be procured enter the schoolroom. And third, that it is the duty of the teacher in governing his school to exhaust all the higher motives and agencies that he can command; but if these should in any case prove unavailing, he may then lawfully resort to corporal punishment as the supplement of all the rest.

What did the long, wordy "Battle of the Books" accomplish? The *Answer* effectively closed the controversy, which had attracted much attention and made a deep impression upon the public mind. The consensus was that Mann had won. The result in the end was a wave of changes which brought about most of the reforms advocated by Mann; corporal punishment in the schools was severely restricted; the standards for qualified teachers were raised; a number of the most incompetent Boston schoolmasters were ousted from their posts; and public attention was focused on the schools to a far greater degree than in the past. Justification for the use of the rod in the name of religion was discredited.

Mann himself was convinced that the principals' attack on him had been inspired by religious fanatics "who think it is necessary first to put me down, that they may afterwards carry out their plans of introducing doctrines into our schools." As he saw the situation, "an extensive conspiracy is now formed to break down the Board of Education, as a preliminary measure to teaching sectarianism in the schools." And doubtless some of the masters *were* motivated by a sectarian point of view, especially in the matter of discipline, arguing, as they did in the *Rejoinder,* that "all authority is of God and must be obeyed" and viewing themselves as God's chosen instruments to exercise physical compulsion, since children were innately evil and must be taught to obey.

The masters' and teachers' opposition to Mann was one of the forces leading to the founding of the Massachusetts Teachers' Association in 1844. Through this device, the Boston principals had hoped and expected to make statewide the fight against Mann, the Board of Education, and their policies. The scheme collapsed before it could get off the ground. At its first session, the Association received a resolution of support for the Board, on which no action was taken, but at its next meeting a resolution was adopted disclaiming any intention of "antagonizing the Board of Education." Benjamin Greenleaf declared that the Association meant "peace on earth, and goodwill to Mann."

In at least one important respect the long-drawn-out squabble served a useful purpose. From there on, Mann received steadily increasing popular support and the lively debate helped to fix his place in history by giving wide currency to his educational beliefs and theories.

An article by William E. Drake offers a penetrating analysis: "It may seem strange to us today that the schoolmasters should have been one of the main sources of opposition to Horace Mann's free schools; yet, on second thought, their position is quite clear. They had been trained in a classical-theological atmosphere; and such training embodied stern devotion to a social and intellectual aristocracy. They were rigid, moral disciplinarians, promiscuously wielding the rod when other means proved ineffective, and lacking any deep-seated humanitarianism toward common men."[60]

CHAPTER 11

The Value of Education

In April, 1836, Massachusetts enacted a law "for the better instruction of youth, employed in manufacturing establishments." The law went into effect almost simultaneously with Horace Mann's appointment as Secretary of the Board of Education. In his *Third Annual Report* Mann notes that in his travels around the state he gave "special attention to the observance or non-observance of the law." The chief provisions of the act were that "no owner, agent, or superintendent of any manufacturing establishment, shall employ any child, under the age of fifteen years, to labor in such establishment, unless such child shall have attended some public or private day school, where instruction is given by a legally qualified teacher, at least three months of the twelve months, not preceding any and every year, in which such child shall be so employed." The penalty for each violation was fifty dollars.

Opposition to the new law, sometimes virulent, came from two sources: the poor and certain manufacturing interests. The illiterate, poverty-stricken masses saw education not as a means to improve their lot or to open new opportunities to their children but as a diabolical scheme to deprive them of their children's labor. "It was found," wrote Mann, "that children could be profitably employed in many kinds of labor,—in factories, in the shoemaking business, and in other mechanical employments; and this swelled the already enormous amount of non-attendance and irregularity." Too frequently, parents regarded their children simply as property and valued them by no higher standard than the money they could earn.

Three years after enactment of the child labor-education law, Mann concluded that in the great majority of cases, the law was being "uniformly and systematically disregarded." It was best observed in the largest manufacturing communities. Violations of the law were most common among private individuals and small corporations. The latter were often fly-by-night concerns which rented space for short periods, tried to realize maximum profits, and then moved on.

Mann blamed the parents as much as the soulless corporations for this state of affairs. "It is obvious," he points out, "that the consent of two parties is necessary to the infraction of this law, and to the infliction of this highest species of injustice upon the children whom it was designed to protect." There were many parents, both among immigrants and the native population, who went from town to town seeking employment for their children. The inevitable consequences of such open defiance of the law, in Mann's view, were that "The neighborhood or town where the law is broken will soon become the receptacle of the poorest, most vicious and abandoned parents, who are bringing up their children to be also as poor, vicious and abandoned as themselves." Mann continued, "Every breach of this law, therefore, inflicts direct and positive injustice, not only upon the children employed, but upon all the industrious and honest communities in which they are employed; because its effect will be to fill those communities with paupers and criminals."[61]

As Mann was writing, Massachusetts had become the greatest manufacturing state in the Union, and industry was in a constant state of expansion. With the growth of a large laboring population, Mann warned that the manufacturing centers could suffer the fate of Manchester, England, where great numbers of the workers "live in the filthiest streets." The remedy was preventive laws, strictly enforced, "to see that no cupidity, no contempt of the public welfare for the sake of private gain, is allowed openly to violate them or clandestinely to evade them."

Frequent references are made in Mann's *Reports* to the alarming rate of absences, nonattendance, and tardiness among school-age children, whether to work in factories or for other reasons. For the school year 1846-47, for example, a total of 204,436 children were supposed to be dependent upon the common schools for their education. Of this number, the average attendance for the summer term was 123,046 and in the winter term 143,878. In other words, there was an average absence during the summer of 81,390 and during the winter of 60,558 pupils. The situation drew complaints from the teachers, whose labors were increased and success diminished by absences; from parents who sent their children to school regularly, because the tardy and infrequent attendees were "a dead weight upon the progress of those who are uniformly present and prompt"; from school committees "because it lowers the general standard of intelligence among the people" and "incurs a total loss of from one third to one half of all the money which is annually levied for the support of schools"; and from the taxpayers, who saw their taxes being wasted because of the children's failure to attend school.

How account for the extremely high level of absences? It was claimed by some parents that they depended partially upon the labor of their children for the support of their families, and they were too poor to sacrifice these earnings, even for the period of the school year. Mann acknowledged that in a few instances "the number or age of the family, sickness, misfortune, or other cause, may render this or some other resource indispensable to the procurement of the necessaries and decencies of life." In other instances, however, "It is well known that a class of parents exists amongst us, who work their children that they themselves may be idle; who coin the health, the capacities and the future welfare of their own offspring into money, which money, when gained, is not expended for the necessaries or the comforts of life, but is wasted upon appetites that brutify or demonize their possessor"[62]—doubtless a reference to Mann's strong aversion to alcohol.

Where cases of genuine need existed, Mann urged public welfare assistance, which would thus free the children of the poor to attend school. The selfish, self-indulgent parents should be "obliged to be industrious, even though coerced by the goads of hunger and cold."

To a missionary for public education, such as Horace Mann, any interference with the educational processes was intolerable. Unnecessary absences were in this category. Education was a universal panacea in Mann's mind, for he felt it had been proved that "if all our children were to be brought under the benignant influences of such teachers as the State can supply, from the age of four years to that of sixteen, and for ten months in each year, ninety-nine in every hundred of them can be rescued from uncharitableness, from falsehood, from intemperance, from cupidity, licentiousness, violence, and fraud, and reared to the performance of all the duties, and the practice of all the kindnesses and courtesies of domestic and social life.[63]

For the materialistic-minded, the practical businessman, the industrialists, and manufacturer, who were inclined to be skeptical of such broad claims, and who asked for concrete evidence of the value of education. Mann was ready. He recognized that it was well to appeal to self-interest and he was therefore constantly endeavoring to prove that educated labor was far more productive and profitable than illiterate labor. Opposition to the improvement of the public schools came mainly, Mann observed, from a "few wealthy leaders, with many times more than their own number of ignorant and deluded followers." Mann directed his appeals, consequently, to men of substance, certain that if they could be convinced, his cause was won. The money expended for education, he maintained, should "be viewed in its true character, as seed-grain sown in a soil which is itself enriched by yielding."

Prior to Mann, advocates of education had emphasized its refining, humanizing aspects, rarely if ever attempting to show its pecuniary worth, both to individuals and to society. "They have not deigned to show," Mann says, "how it can raise more abundant harvests, and multiply the conveniences of domestic life; how it can build, transport, manufacture, mine, navigate, fortify." He had evidence, Mann believed, "to prove that education is convertible into houses and lands, as well as into power and virtue." He offers no apologies for this utilitarian view of education. Nature dictates that in order to survive, mankind requires food, raiment, and shelter. Moreover, "No hungry or houseless people ever were, or ever will be, an intelligent or a moral one." Mann goes on:

I proceed then to show that education has a power of ministering to our personal and material wants beyond all other agencies, whether excellence of climate, spontaneity of production, mineral resources, or mines of silver and gold. Every wise parent and community, desiring the prosperity of their children, even in the most wordly sense, will spare no pains in giving them a generous education.

Extensive statistics were compiled by Mann to clinch his argument that "education has a market value; that it is so far an article of merchandise, that it may be turned to a pecuniary account: it may be minted, and will yield a larger amount of statutable coin than common bullion." He carried on a wide correspondence and "held personal interviews with many of the most practical, sagacious and intelligent business men amongst us, who for many years have had large numbers of persons in their employment." Mann's aim was to determine the difference in productive ability between the educated and the uneducated. For this purpose, he "conferred and corresponded with manufacturers of all kinds, with machinists, engineers, railroad contractors, officers in the army, etc."

For some types of labor, Mann acknowledged that comparisons are difficult, if not impossible.

But when hundreds of men or women work side by side, in the same factory, at the same machinery, in making the same fabrics, and by a fixed rule of the establishment, labor the same number of hours each day; and when, also, the products of each operative can be counted in number, weighed by the pound, or measured by the yard or cubic foot,—then it is perfectly practicable to determine with arithmetical exactness the productions of one individual and one class as compared with those of another individual or class.[64]

In compliance with Mann's request, a number of manufacturers examined their books for a series of years to ascertain the quality and quantity of work performed by persons in their employ. The result of the investigation revealed, Mann reports, "a most astonishing superiority in productive power, on the part of the educated over the uneducated laborer." When guided by an intelligent mind, the hand becomes a different instrument. Processes were performed both more rapidly and better by workers with a good common school education. Furthermore, their promotions permit them to "rise to a higher and higher point, in the kinds of labor performed, and also in the rate of wages paid, while the ignorant sink, like dregs, and are always found at the bottom."

Mann's circular letter mailed out to those from whom he solicited information and opinions was a long document, fully explaining the reasons for the inquiry and his objectives. At the outset, it is observed that numerous men of wealth and leisure were indifferent or even hostile to the cause of common education, because they "profess to fear that a more thorough and comprehensive education for the whole people, will destroy contentment, loosen habits of industry, engender a false ambition, and prompt to an incursion into their own favored sphere." Mann then goes on to ask a number of searching questions of the employers, directed especially at discovering differences in individuals growing out of differences in their educational background.

The letter concludes with a semiapology, stating that of course the person addressed realizes the importance of education and favors support for the common schools, and it may be considered superfluous for him to reply to such an inquiry. On the other hand, "while we have influential persons, who dwell with us in the same common mansions of society, and who, having secured for themselves a few well-lighted apartments, now insist that total darkness is better for a portion of the occupants born and dwelling under the same roof . . . it is necessary to adduce facts and arguments, and to present motives, which shall prove both to the blinded and those who would keep them so, the value and beauty of light."

The response to Mann's inquiry produced "a mass of facts," he reported. Several letters were included verbatim in the *Fifth Annual Report.*[65]

One was from James K. Mills, of Boston, whose company employed about three thousand persons in cotton mills, machine shops, and calico printing works. On the basis of personal observation and experience, Mills had reached three conclusions: first, "the rudiments of a Common School education are essential to the attainment of skill and expertness as laborers, or to consideration and respect in the civil and social relations of life"; second, "very few, who have not enjoyed the advantages of a Common

School education, ever rise above the lowest class of operatives"; and, third, "a large majority of the overseers, and other employed in situations which require a high degree of skill, in particular branches; which, oftentimes, require a good general knowledge of business, and *always,* an unexceptionable moral character, have made their way up from the condition of common laborers, with no other advantage over a large proportion of those they have left behind, than that derived from a better education." Mills went on to express the belief that the best cotton mill in New England would, if manned only by illiterate operatives, never yield the proprietor a profit and its machinery would soon be worn out. "I cannot imagine any situation in life," he states, "where the want of a Common School education would be more severely felt, or be attended with worse consequences than in our manufacturing villages."

A second letter was from H. Bartlett, a Lowell manufacturer employing from 400 to 900 persons. Bartlett had found the best educated to be the most profitable help, "those who have a good Common School education giving, as a class, invariably, a better production than those brought up in ignorance." Further, the better educated made the best wages, had the most order and system, kept their machinery in better order, were less inclined to agitation and violence, and were more moral in their behavior. There was no question in Bartlett's mind that "the owners of manufacturing property have a deep pecuniary interest in the education and morals of their help." As competition among manufacturers became keener, "the establishment, other things being equal, which has the best educated and the most moral help, will give the greatest production at the least cost per pound." Lowell's preeminence as a manufacturing center was attributed by Bartlett to the fact that the city had "23 public schools, 15 churches, and numerous associations for intellectual improvement."

The Mills-Bartlett statements were fully supported by John Clark, also of Lowell, superintendent of Merrimack Mills, who "found, with very few exceptions, the best educated among my hands to be the most capable, intelligent, energetic, industrious, economical and moral; they produce the best work, and the most of it, with the least injury to the machinery." In terms of wages, the best educated of Clark's 1,500 operatives were paid about eighteen percent above the general average in the mills, and about forty percent above the wages of a group who were unable to write their names.

A substantial portion of Mann's *Fifth Annual Report* is devoted to his findings on the pecuniary benefits of education. It presents a direct and convincing appeal to industrialists to support the public schools. Some 18,000 copies were circulated by the New York legislature, it was translated into German, and it was often cited in educational periodicals and in speeches delivered by educational leaders. It demonstrated persuasively, as one of Mann's correspondents stated, that "the aim of industry is served, and the wealth of the country is augmented, in proportion to the diffusion of knowledge." The concept of the money value of education was not completely new in Mann's time, but he was the first to popularize the idea and to assemble strong supporting evidence. Writing in 1860, a distinguished educator, John D. Philbrick, observed that the *Fifth Annual Report* had "probably done more than all other publications written within the past twenty-five years to convince capitalists of the value of elementary education as a means of increasing the value of labor."

Though the wealthy paid lip service to education, even Mann's eloquent appeals to them for contributions to support schools and the general cause of education went largely unheeded, except for Edward Dwight's aid in founding the first normal schools. Others found various excuses for not donating funds. Mann, disappointed and disillusioned, was gradually drawn toward socialistic notions for sharing the wealth of the world.

Striking illustrations are used by Mann in demonstrating the practical utility of education. For example, assume that a workman is employed to move blocks of squared granite, each weighing 1,080 pounds. Without mechanical aids, several laborers exerting a force equal to 758 pounds are required to move a block any distance. Placed on rollers on a wooden platform, only 22 pounds of force are needed. Since the invention of locomotives and railroads, a 1,080-pound body could be moved with a draft of three or four pounds. In short, the application of intelligence had reduced the force necessary to move a massive body by two hundred times. Another equally arresting example is offered:

If a savage will learn how to swim, he can fasten a dozen pounds' weight on his back, and transport it across a narrow river, or other body of water of moderate width. If he will invent an axe, or other instrument, by which to cut down a tree, he can use the tree for a float, and one of its limbs for a paddle, and can thus transport many times the former weight, many times the former distance. . . .Fastening several trees together, he makes a raft, and thus increases the buoyant power of his embryo water-craft.[66]

Mann then goes on to describe succeeding steps which eventually produce a *ship-shape* craft, afterwards a merchantman sailing ship, and finally a steamship, a creation which "cleaves oceans, breasts tides, defies tempests, and bears its living and jubilant freight around the globe."

The tremendous rate of progress in the mechanical and useful arts, characteristic of recent times, had been slow to get under way, Mann concludes, because "the labor of the world was performed by ignorant men," and it was not until "some degree of intelligence dawned upon the workman" that improvements were made. The number of intelligent, educated individuals was small and concentrated in a limited geographical area. "The middle classes of England, and the people of Holland and Scotland, have done a hundred times more" to bring about improvements, asserts Mann, "than all the eastern hemisphere besides. What single improvement in art, or discovery in science," he asks, "has ever originated in Spain, or throughout the vast empire of the Russians?" Discoveries and inventions have increased in number and importance in direct proportion to the number of educated, intelligent minds, Mann finds, and the "progression has been geometrical rather than arithmetical," as bright minds react upon one another, "for the action of the mind is like the action of fire."

Poverty was seen by Mann as a public and private evil. There is no reason for its existence. "Cold, hunger, and nakedness are not, like death, an inevitable lot"; "the earth contains abundant resources for ten times—doubtless for twenty times—its present inhabitants." Single states in the Union were capable of producing enough food for all, or of growing enough cotton to clothe the whole nation, or of mining enough coal to warm every house to a reasonable temperature for centuries to come. Only an unequal distribution of wealth prevents the elimination of poverty. The

Commonwealth of Massachusetts was founded, according to Mann, on the theory that "all are to have an equal chance for earning, and equal security in the enjoyment of what they earn." In actuality, "the distance between the two extremes is lengthening, instead of being abridged"; the rich were getting richer and the poor were becoming poorer. Because of its highly industrialized base, Massachusetts was vulnerable "far beyond any other state in the Union, to the fatal extremes of overgrown wealth and desperate poverty."

Nothing except universal education, in Mann's estimation, could counteract the trend toward the domination of capital and the servility of labor. If education could be made widespread, no "intelligent and practical body of men should be permanently poor." Mann adds: "Education, then, beyond all other devices of human origin, is the great equalizer of the conditions of men,—the balance-wheel of the social machinery." Education does not necessarily elevate man's moral nature, but "it gives each man the independence and the means by which he can resist the selfishness of other men."

In his twelfth and final *Annual Report,* Mann presents in eloquent and resounding phrases his educational credo, his almost sublime faith in the magic power of education:

For the creation of wealth, then—for the existence of a wealthy people and a wealthy nation,—intelligence is the grand condition. The number of improvers will increase as the intellectual constituency, if I may so call it, increases. In former times, and in most parts of the world even at the present day, not one man in a million has ever had such a development of mind as made it possible for him to become a contributor to art or science. Let this development precede, and contributions, numberless, and of inestimable value, will be sure to follow. That political economy, therefore, which busies itself about capital and labor, supply and demand, interest and rents, favorable balances of trade, but leaves out of account the element of a widespread mental development, is nought but stupendous folly. The greatest of all the arts in political economy is to change a consumer into a producer; and the next greatest is to increase the producer's producing power,—an end to be directly attained by increasing his intelligence. For mere delving, an ignorant man is but little better than a swine, whom he so much resembles in his appetites, and surpasses in his powers of mischief.[67]

CHAPTER 12

Influence at Home and Abroad

In his *Ninth Annual Report,* Horace Mann notes that "not a week passes, from one end of the year to the other, when we are not called upon, by leading men of other states and countries, to give information respecting the organization, the administration and the success of our schools."

Mann's influence in stimulating an educational renaissance was by no means limited to Massachusetts. His fame was country-wide. Virtually every state in the Union felt the impact of his ideas. When James Wadsworth wished to contribute a large sum of money to the New York schools, in 1841, he wrote to ask Mann's advice, as a result of which the textbook on teaching by Emerson and Potter was distributed free to each teacher in the New York system. On another occasion, when New York sought a principal for the newly established normal school in Albany, the selection committee conferred with Mann and, on his advice, appointed David P. Page. At Henry Barnard's request, Mann went to Hartford while the legislature was in session and paved the way for the creation of the Connecticut Board of School Commissioners. One of Mann's addresses at Providence, Rhode Island, was responsible for the establishment of the city's high school. A committee appointed by the Maryland legislature to plan a system of common schools for the state carried on correspondence with Mann in order to learn details of the Massachusetts system.

Mann was popular as a public speaker and he addressed innumerable teachers' institutes in Massachusetts, New York, and

Ohio. When Iowa set out to organize an educational system, Mann was asked to serve as a member of the planning committee. At the invitation of the Indiana State Teachers Association, he spoke to that body on "The Duty of the State to Provide for and Control the Education of Youth." The first session of the Missouri State Teachers Association was addressed by Mann and his visit to St. Louis led to the establishment of a normal school there. In the neighboring state of Illinois, Mann was speaker for the State Teachers Association's second annual session. The University of Michigan's Board of Regents asked for advice in choosing a chancellor.

Less well known than Mann's impact on educational developments in New England, the Middle Atlantic states, and the Midwest was his influence on the Southern states. A leading educational historian, Edgar W. Knight, has thoroughly documented the effects of Mann's public school philosophy on the states from Louisiana to Virginia.[68] Southern interest in his ideas and accomplishments was particularly noticeable after his European trip in 1843 and the publication in the same year of his famous report on European, and especially Prussian, schools. Contemporary records reveal, Knight states, that "the common school awakening of the second quarter of the past century was not confined exclusively to any part of the country." Prior to Mann's debut, reports on educational matters by Victor Cousin, Calvin Stowe, Archibald D. Murphey, Benjamin M. Smith, and others had been widely circulated and helped to stir interest in schools at home and abroad.

Most familiar of all the reports, however, were those written by Horace Mann. Mann's struggle against numerous obstacles to upgrade education in Massachusetts had been closely followed by Southern leaders and educational pioneers, who had high respect for the New Englander's diligence, tenacity, and outstanding achievements. The chief evidence offered by Knight is Mann's correspondence with people in the Southern states who knew about his work, were reading his reports and speeches, and sought his advice on educational matters. Between 1839 and 1850, Mann received letters from a host of people and fraternal organizations, asking for information on education in New England, especially in Massachusetts, and similar issues. The letters came from every Southern state except Arkansas and Texas, with the largest representation from Mississippi and Virginia.

Among the personal letters which came to Mann from Southerners, several of special interest and significance may be cited. William H. Gray wrote from Leesburg, Virginia, August 31, 1845, stating that the people of his county were discussing "the propriety of adopting, in lieu of the present, the Common School system" and asked for information on the subject. Gray had seen some of Mann's reports and desired others, especially the famous *Seventh Annual Report.* On November 7, 1845, John W. Forbes wrote from Fredericksburg to say that about a month later a convention was to be held in Richmond to consider the best means for promoting the education of all classes in Virginia. The convention would be composed of representatives "appointed by primary assemblies of the people of most if not all of the counties of this Commonwealth." Forbes wrote that it would be "eminently desirable to have as much and as accurate information in regard to the school systems in other states as possible," and he knew of no one better qualified than Mann to supply such information. Forbes asked for a copy of the law which had established the public school system in Massachusetts, together with any suggestions and publications helpful to the people of Virginia. Another Virginian, R.B. Gooch, a member of the convention's committee to devise and recommend a system of education for Virginia, wrote from Richmond at approximately the same time with a similar inquiry. Gooch had heard of Mann's reputation "on the other side of the Atlantic." He observed that the assembly would "have many opponents and apathy to contend with," as well as a sparsity of population and conflicting views among the people about the best way to establish a common school system. Anything from Mann's pen, "whether of argument or fact," Gooch promised, "will receive the attentive ear of the Convention." Gooch also asked for advice on starting an educational periodical, such as Mann's *Common School Journal.*

Mann was meticulous in responding to all serious inquiries, no matter how time-consuming. Unfortunately, his correspondents were less careful to preserve his replies than he was to save their letters. His answer to Gooch, which has survived, urged *state* rather than *county* taxation for educational purposes, arguing that those who needed "an improved system least, would be the only ones which would adopt it, while with those who needed it most, their indifference would be proportionate to their need. As in the body, if the healthy parts do not aid the diseased, the latter will soon run to corruption." Mann went on to point out that "selfish considerations" are generally against educational improvements, the ignorant are not "alarmed at their ignorance," and are justly punished for their indifference, but sadly, "this punishment is inflicted upon the innocent quite as much as upon the guilty." In the Gooch letter, Mann discussed the "relative importance" of the lower schools and of higher educational institutions. It could be depended upon as "a law of nature," wrote Mann, "that colleges and academies will never act downwards to raise the mass of the people by education; but on the contrary, common schools will feed and sustain the academies and colleges. Heat ascends, and it will warm upwards, but it will not warm downwards." Mann also urged the Virginians to appoint a state superintendent of the common schools and to make provisions for the education of teachers. "All the money in the world, without a higher grade of teachers than you can now command," he declared, "will never raise your schools to any elevated standards."

As for starting an educational journal, Mann was not encouraging in his letter to Gooch. Only an able editor and subscribers who would provide sustained support could guarantee the success of such a venture. Mann had edited the *Common School Journal* "for now seven years as a labour of love—that is, for nothing; and it has hardly defrayed the printer's bills."

Henry Ruffner, father of William H. Ruffner, Virginia's first superintendent of public schools, wrote to Mann from Lexington on August 13, 1848, thanking him for "copies of your speech and report on education," agreed with the sentiments expressed, and wished that he "had a thousand copies" to distribute in his state and Kentucky. The elder Ruffner had prepared and presented to the Virginia legislature a report pointing out the defects of the state's educational system and proposing adoption of advanced ideas and methods in public educational organization, administration, and support, and normal schools and other provisions for the education of teachers. The school system established in Virginia in 1869-70 was set up by William H. Ruffner on principles outlined in his father's report nearly three decades earlier, which in turn had been greatly influenced by Horace Mann's writings and work in Massachusetts.

Mann's reports had also stirred up much interest in Mississippi. A number of letters in the Mann archives request advice and help, copies of publications, etc. Governor A. G. Brown, a strong supporter of education, was apparently directly influenced by Mann's example. Before his election as governor, Brown had urged the establishment of public free schools for all the children of the state, made an eloquent plea for public education in his 1844 inaugural address, and persuaded the legislature in 1846 to enact legislation providing for the first general system of public schools in Mississippi.

Mann's correspondence file contains communications on educational matters also from Alabama, Florida, Georgia, North and South Carolina, Louisiana, and Tennessee. The letters deal with such common problems as the lack of adequate public schools, the indifference to education of most citizens, the question of education for women, the shortage of funds, and teacher preparation.

George B. Emerson, writing in 1844, summed up the impact which Mann was making on his contemporaries in the educational field:

Mann's reports have worked an echo in the woods of Maine, on the banks of the St. Lawrence, on the shores of the Great Lakes. They have been read and listened to in New York, in the West and Southwest. The importance they have acquired is shown by the fact that a man from Massachusetts has been selected to organize the schools of New Orleans. At this very moment his reports are regenerating the Rhode Island schools, while in the remotest corners of Ohio forty people have been known to meet to read together the only copy of the Boston secretary's reports which they had been able to obtain.

Abroad, the most celebrated cases of Mann's influence were in Latin America, especially in Chile and Argentina, exerted through an exiled Argentine, Domingo Faustino Sarmiento.[69] The Latin American nations naturally looked to Europe for leadership and in 1845 Sarmiento was commissioned by a Chilean educational leader to study the state of primary education in

European countries, preparatory to developing a Chilean national school system. The following year was spent by Sarmiento visiting Spain, Italy, France, Germany, Switzerland, and England. He found much to criticize in the Spanish and French school systems, but praised the Prussian state educational organization, as had Mann three years earlier. From Prussia, Sarmiento crossed the Channel to London and spent several months examining the English way of life.

While in London, Sarmiento came across a copy of Mann's *Report of an Educational Tour in Germany, France, Holland, and Parts of Great Britain and Ireland*. The reading of the report was a major event in Sarmiento's life and for Latin America. "After this important work fell into my hands," Sarmiento wrote, "I had a fixed point to which to direct myself in the United States." He had to get to know "the only great and powerful Republic on the face of the earth," as he described the United States, though his primary purpose was to visit Horace Mann. On October 1, 1847, Sarmiento knocked on Mann's door in West Newton, Massachusetts, was invited in, and spent the next two days talking about education.

Mann and Sarmiento had no language in common, but fortunately Mary Mann and the Argentine were both fluent in French. With Mrs. Mann acting as interpreter, Sarmiento received simple, practical answers to every kind of query he could conceive concerning the operation of a school system. "In long hours of conference on two successive days," according to Sarmiento's record, he received information and inspiration from "this noble promoter of education garnered in the intimacy which our common sympathies established [including] a thousand useful facts which I have used to great advantage." The liberal views of the two men coincided at almost every point, and their practical aims were identical. The Argentine regarded Mann as "the St. Paul of Education."

Sarmiento was supplied by Mann with letters of introduction to Ralph Waldo Emerson, Henry Wadsworth Longfellow (with whom he conversed in Spanish), and prominent government officials. During the course of his stay, he visited twenty-one states, admiring, comparing, and learning. As he traveled about, the country made a tremendous impression upon him, marred by only one great flaw—slavery. Sarmiento could see no solution to this social and racial evil other than war between North and South.

Sarmiento returned to Chile in 1848 with the deepest admiration for the practical Boston school leader. "To an inexhaustible fund of goodness and philanthropy," he wrote, "Horace Mann unites in his acts and his writings a rare prudence and a profound knowledge." From that time on, Sarmiento no longer looked to Europe for leadership in educational administration. To Mann he gave credit for creating a state-wide system of education that would insure continuing improvement in the United States. After digesting the ideas absorbed from Horace Mann and from his travel observations, Sarmiento wrote an influential and popular book, *De la Educación Comun,* published in 1849, presenting the case for free tax-supported education for all. During the following five years he produced a stream of articles on the subject of schools and libraries. The principles which he advocated again and again, all of which would have been endorsed by Horace Mann, were support for education from a tax specifically levied for school purposes; the education of girls, including the training of 2,000 women as elementary school teachers; establishment of normal schools and kindergartens; school buildings based upon American designs and equipped with artificial ventilation, blackboards, and desks; the adoption of American penmanship and American script in writing and more attention to the art of reading; and gymnastics in a physical education program.

Argentina's future president championed public, school, and regional libraries, and proposed that governments should take the lead in distributing useful books. Sarmiento and Mann differed on the subject of fiction. The latter considered the reading of fiction undesirable, if not actually harmful. Sarmiento's view was that it is unfortunate many readers limit themselves chiefly to novels, but this is preferable to not reading at all.

Sarmiento remained in Chile until 1855. During those years he drafted the law which founded the Chilean elementary school system, established normal schools, and through his writings created a strong spirit for improved schools. Except for a brief period in 1852, he had lived continuously abroad in a self-imposed exile since 1841. Shortly after his return to Argentina,

Sarmiento was appointed to the newly created post of Minister of Education. In that position, which he filled until 1862, he entered with complete dedication and tremendous enthusiasm into the work of organizing a public school system and popular libraries. In 1862, Sarmiento was elected governor of his native province of San Juan, and immediately instituted a reform program there. He began by making public education obligatory, erected a model school, and improved public administration.

Partly for political reasons, Sarmiento was appointed Argentine Minister in Washington, giving him an opportunity for a return visit to the United States. When he arrived in Washington in 1865, he discovered that far-reaching events and changes had taken place during his absence. The Civil War had just ended, slavery had been abolished, Abraham Lincoln had been assassinated, and the new President, Andrew Johnson, faced a hostile Congress. During the next three years, Sarmiento devoted himself to the study of American institutions, visited various kinds of organizations, including teachers' associations, and acquainted himself with the American social and political structure. His respect for American educational methods and American democracy remained undiminished.

Sarmiento had not been long in his new post when he read that a statue of Horace Mann had been erected on the State House grounds in Boston. Mann had died six years earlier (1859). Sarmiento at once wrote a laudatory letter to Mary Mann, beginning a friendship and frequent correspondence which continued until Mrs. Mann's death in 1887, a year before Sarmiento's. In 1865, Sarmiento again visited the Mann home, and while there met the most distinguished literary and educational figures of the time in Boston and Cambridge. Subsequently, Mary Mann translated one of Sarmiento's books into English, wrote his biography, and selected the first American teachers to go to Argentina.

While absent in the United States, Sarmiento was nominated and elected President of the Argentine Republic. He returned home without delay and was inaugurated on October 12, 1868. Two beautiful marble busts of Horace Mann and Abraham Lincoln were carried back with him, works of art which he had commissioned from the sculptor William Rimmer, a Mann relative. Sarmiento's administration was marked by great progress in primary education throughout Argentina, new schools were created by public taxation, and libraries were founded to improve general culture. Following his retirement from the presidency in 1874, Sarmiento accepted the post of Director General of Schools in Buenos Aires Province, where he continued active promotion of education and libraries.

Sarmiento's continued admiration for his mentor is attested to by the fact that after returning to Argentina he translated Mary Mann's *Life of Horace Mann* into Spanish. When Mann's writings were published, he wrote, "If I could give any advice to South American governments, this would be that they should procure the greatest possible number of copies of that work and scatter them freely in every city and village."

Another Latin American nation, Uruguay, also felt Horace Mann's influence, though less directly. José Pedro Varela, the great Uruguayan educator, visited the United States in 1868. Inspired by what he observed there and by his acquaintance with Sarmiento, Varela, as head of the Commission of Public Instruction in Montevideo, sponsored reform bills which incorporated American educational ideas and systems. His contributions to education came principally from Mann, as evidence of which Varela was popularly known as "The Horace Mann of Uruguay."

Mann's fame spread to Europe as well as to Latin America. The governments of Germany and Great Britain reprinted his reports for circulation in those countries. The *Seventh Annual Report* was "read with admiration in the highest circles abroad," according to a statement by the U.S. Commissioner of Education in 1897. Even the London *Athenaeum,* usually hostile to anything American, as noted earlier, had a complimentary review.

Mann's admirers were especially numerous in France, where his political, social, and anticlerical views were in accord with the rising spirit of republicanism after the fall of Napoleon III. Félix Pecaut, writing in 1888, commended Mann's system of moral teaching. *The Work and Writings of Horace Mann,* translated by M. J. Gaufrès, was published in 1888 for the Musée Pédagogique in its *Educational Memoirs and Documents.* Long after his death, Mann continued to exert a strong influence upon the development of the French schools' civic morality curriculum. Gabriel Compayré in his *Horace Mann and the Public School in the United States* concludes the work with this tribute to Mann:

It may be said also that his spirit has penetrated into Europe and particularly into France. It will not be detracting from the honor due to the organizers of elementary instruction in France under the Third Republic to say that they were in great measure inspired by the thought and example of the great American educator.[70]

CHAPTER 13

National Statesman

On February 25, 1848, John Quincy Adams, ex-President, who was rounding out a notable career as a member of the House of Representatives, suddenly died, of a stroke, shortly after responding to a roll call. His death was to have an immediate impact on Horace Mann's future.

To friends' suggestion that he should be a candidate to succeed Adams, Mann responded modestly: "To ask anybody in this district to fill Mr. Adams's place is a good deal like asking a mouse to fill an elephant's skin." Nevertheless, when he was offered the nomination by the Whigs, he accepted, and was elected by a majority of 904 votes. Mann was motivated in making the decision by several factors: the belief that the common school cause in Massachusetts was so firmly established that "nothing could overturn it"; the possibility that as a member of Congress he would be in a strong position to carry on his education crusade for the nation as a whole, perhaps in time becoming national Secretary of Education; and the fact that his personal finances were in a critical state, due mainly to unwise loans and too generous donations to the Massachusetts school system. Mann took the oath of office in the nation's capital on April 13, 1848.

The state of Massachusetts gave concrete expression to its appreciation for Mann's immense labors on behalf of its schools when the legislature voted an appropriation of two thousand dollars in "partial payment," to recompense Mann for his out-of-pocket contributions to the normal schools and other projects. In the meantime, Mann completed his Board of Education duties by writing a final article for the *Common School Journal* and submitting his *Twelfth Annual Report,* his last.

John Quincy Adams had been an indefatigable champion of the abolition movement, had waged war against the spread of the slavery system, and had fought all attempts to subvert the right of petition and freedom of speech on the highly controversial subject. Slavery remained the dominant theme in all congressional debate. Among the great orators currently holding forth in the legislative halls were Webster, Calhoun, Clay, Benton, Douglas, Chase, Seward, Alexander Stevens, and other men of like caliber.

As a mere freshman in Congress, Horace Mann remained quiet for several months. The term was well under way when he entered Congress. As he wrote to Charles Sumner, who was prodding him to take strong stands on slavery and other current issues, "I came into the class here when the other members of it had read the book half through; so that I had the back lessons all to make up." For one with Mann's unyielding convictions on freedom and slavery and notable oratorical abilities, however, it would have been unnatural to remain in the background for any extended period.

As it turned out, all of Mann's five major speeches and most of his energies while a member of the House were devoted to the slavery issue. The title of his first address, delivered on June 30, 1848, was "Slavery in the Territories." The chamber was packed, with friends and foes, eager to hear the views of the famous Massachusetts educator and orator. At the outset, contrary to the arguments of Southern leaders, Mann cited many legal precedents to show that Congress had a clear right to legislate on the subject of slavery for the territories, and furthermore had the duty to exclude slavery from them. From the legal he turned to the economic aspects. "So far from facilitating the increase of individual or national wealth," Mann asserted, "slavery retards both. It blasts worldly prosperity. Other things being equal, a free people will thrive and prosper, in a mere worldly sense, more than a people divided into masters and slaves." Developing the argument further, Mann stated, "Enslave a man, and you destroy his ambition, his enterprise, his capacity." Any wealth created by the slave is seized by his owner and no matter how "industrious

and frugal he may be, he has nothing to bequeath to his children."
Only fear, not hope, makes him work. To compare slave labor to
free labor, asserted Mann, is to compare the horse to the locomo-
tive.

An unfortunate side effect of slavery, Mann went on to observe, is that it makes white labor disreputable, and therefore
shunned. "The pecuniary loss resulting from this," he noted, "is
incalculable." The community loses in another way: "The slave
must be kept in ignorance. He must not be educated, lest with
education should come a knowledge of his natural rights, and the
means of escape or the power of vengeance." The slaveowner
"abolishes the mighty power of the intellect, and uses only the
weak, degraded, and half-animated forces of the human limbs."
Speaking as one dedicated to the value and importance of education, Mann pointed out that "the most abundant proof exists,
derived from all departments of human industry, that uneducated labor is comparatively unprofitable labor." The prohibition
against educating the blacks is disastrous, too, because "slavery
makes the general education of the whites impossible." Harking
back to his Massachusetts experience, Mann maintained that "you
cannot have general education without Common Schools. Common Schools cannot exist where the population is sparse. . . .It is
impossible to have free and universal education in a slave state." A
direct consequence of this situation, Mann stated, using a
governor's message as his authority, was that one-fourth of the
adult free white population of Virginia was unable to read or
write. Statistics were cited to demonstrate that there were eight
times as many pupils in the primary schools of the free states as in
the slave states. New York alone had two and a half times as many,
and Ohio more than equaled the number in the fifteen slave
states and territories.

Other signs of Southern backwardness, to be blamed on the
institution of slavery, were enumerated in detail by Mann. Virtually all the great mechanical inventions had originated in the
North. Patent Office reports showed that six or eight times as
many patents had been taken out for the North as for the South.
Iron manufacture and shipbuilding in the South were only a
fraction of those industries in the North. Fifty times as many

books were printed in the North as in the South. Public, school, college, and university libraries in the North vastly exceeded in number and size those of the South.

Mann concluded his forceful attack by examining the morality of slavery. The institution itself, he said, "is against natural right." There is no justification "for it in the eternal principles of justice and equity. . . . All the noblest instincts of human nature rebel against it." To Mann, slavery was "the most compact, and concentrated, and condensed system of wrong which the depravity of man has ever invented."

The reception of Mann's speech, nearly an hour in length, was predictable. On one hand, his friends and followers, already converted, were warm in their praises; on the other side, hostile and bitter critics, especially from the South, savagely attacked what they considered his misguided, mischievous views, and even his character.

Attempts by the proslavery forces to cut off debate, impose gag rule, and enforce a policy of silence on Congress concerning the slavery issue were defied by Mann, with an impassioned plea for freedom:

I feel nonetheless inclined to discuss this question because an order has gone forth that it shall not be discussed. Discussion has been denounced as agitation, and then it has been dictatorially proclaimed that "agitation must be put down." Humble as I am, I submit to no such dictation, come from what quarter or what numbers it may. . . . In this government, it is not tolerable for any man, however high, or for any body of men, however large, to prescribe what subjects may be agitated, and what may not be agitated. Such prescription is at best but a species of lynch law against free speech. It is as hateful as any other form of that execrable code; and I do but express the common sentiment of all generous minds, when I say that for one, I am all the more disposed to use my privilege of speech, when imperious men, and the sycophants of imperious men, attempt to ban or constrain me. . . . I hold treason against this government to be an enormous crime; but great as it is, I hold treason against free speech and free thought to be a crime incomparably greater.[71]

Horace Mann had scarcely arrived in Washington when he was thrown into another long-drawn-out controversy. On April 16, 1848, Captain Daniel Drayton was indicted for "stealing and carrying away in the schooner Pearl" a cargo of seventy-six slaves from the District of Columbia. Captain Drayton, financed by northern abolitionists, had chartered a small boat, and gone to Washington to help the slaves escape. The vessel was caught in a storm as it sailed down the Potomac, was captured, and Drayton and Edward Sayres, owner of the boat, were brought back to Washington and jailed. Various prominent legal lights—Joshua Giddings, antislavery congressman from Ohio, William Seward, Salmon P. Chase, Benjamin Wade, and others—came forward with offers to defend the prisoners. One by one, however, each withdrew from the case, leaving only Horace Mann as attorney for the defense. The case dragged out through the hot August weather. The first two trials resulted in verdicts of guilty, one after a hearing in a criminal court and the second after a retrial before the circuit court. Armed slaveholders were in court daily. Mann's efforts on behalf of the defendants were continued without reserve. He felt that he was "not working for Drayton and Sayres only but for the whole colored race." Ironically, the relentless district attorney prosecuting the case, Philip Barton Key, was the son of Francis Scott Key, author of "The Star Spangled Banner."

In the end, representing a partial victory, heavy fines were imposed on Drayton and Sayres and they were sentenced "to remain in jail till the bill was paid." Unable to raise the funds, the defendants were held in prison for more than four years, until pardoned by President Fillmore, after which they were hurriedly smuggled north before the state of Virginia could start new prosecutions against them. As for Horace Mann, while he received extensive publicity in connection with the case, his per diem pay in the House was lost while attending court, his bare expenses were paid by the committee which had urged him to accept the case—though all agreed he had performed brilliantly—and he received no fee at all. When finances were concerned, Mann always appeared to come out on the short end.

Mann's second speech in Congress, delivered on February 23, 1849, dealt with slavery and the slave trade in the District of Columbia. "By authority of Congress," he stated, "the city of Washington is the Congo of America," with a flourishing slave market. Within sight of the White House and the Washington

Monument, there were slave pens, "horrid and black receptacles where human beings are penned like cattle, and kept like cattle, that they may be sold like cattle." Mann took particular exception to the breaking up of families which often occurred in the auctions: "the father of a family to go, perhaps, to the rice fields of South Carolina, the mother to the cotton fields of Alabama, and the children to be scattered over the sugar planatations of Louisiana or Texas."

During the preceding fifty years, Mann pointed out, the world had made great progress in the abolition of slavery. The practice had been banned throughout the British Empire and in much of the rest of the world. Only America had stood still during that eventful period. Congress had steadily refused to abolish the slave trade, even in the nation's capital.

A proslavery congressman from Pennsylvania, Richard Brodhead, interrupted Mann's speech to ask, "Would you advance the slaves to an equal social and political condition with the white race?" hoping to trap Mann into a position of supporting miscegenation, to which Mann responded:

I would give to every human being the best opportunity I could to develop and cultivate the faculties which God has bestowed upon him, and which, therefore, he holds under a divine charter. I would take from his neck the heel that has trodden him down; I would dispel from his mind the cloud that has shrouded him in moral night; I would remove the obstructions that have forbidden his soul to aspire; and having done this, I would leave him, as I would leave every other man, to find his level,—to occupy the position to which he should be entitled by his intelligence and his virtues.[72]

To those who feared the evils of miscegenation, Mann expressed doubt that legal amalgamation between the races would ever take place, "unless, in the changed condition of society, reasons shall exist to warrant and sanction it; and in that case, it will carry its own justification with it." Then, probing a highly vulnerable opening in the armor of the slaveholders, Mann commented sarcastically, "But one thing I could never understand,—why those who are so horror-stricken at the idea of *theoretic* amalgamation, should exhibit to the world, in all their cities, on all their plantations, and in all their households, such numberless proofs of *practical* amalgamation." Slavery, he observed, had become "a bedside institution," and "the one race has been to the other, not the object of benevolence, but the victim of licentiousness."

Nearly a year went by before Mann's third speech in the House of Representatives. On February 15, 1850, he addressed Congress again on the subject of slavery in the territories, repeating and expanding upon many of his earlier arguments. In addition, Southern threats to rebel against the federal government or to dissolve the Union over the slavery issue received detailed attention. Widespread sentiment existed among Southern hotheads for secession and for creating a new confederacy—a great slaveholding republic incorporating Cuba and parts of Mexico. Mann accused the South of wanting to rewrite the Declaration of Independence, "as the devil reads Scripture, backwards":

We hold these truths to be self-evident, that men are not created equal; that they are not endowed by their Creator with inalienable rights; that white men, of the Anglo-Saxon race, were born to rob, and tyrannize, and enjoy, and black men, of the African race, to labor, and suffer, and obey.[73]

Secession to form a "United States South," Mann warned (ten years before the outbreak of the Civil War), would lead inevitably to war, in which the South would be the loser. But, he concluded, "under a full sense of my responsibility to my country and my God, I deliberately say, better disunion,—better a civil or servile war,—better any thing that God in his providence shall send, than an extension of the bounds of slavery."

In an endeavor to preserve the Union, Henry Clay presented, on January 27, 1850, a "Compromise" which he hoped would head off civil war. Clay's principal proposals were four in number: admission of California as a state with a constitution prohibiting slavery; the establishment of territorial governments in Utah and New Mexico, leaving the question of slavery to be determined later; granting the South a stringent fugitive slave law which the North must enforce; and abolition of the slave trade in the District of Columbia. Clay warned that no state had the right to secede and predicted "ferocious and bloody" civil war should it be attempted.

About a month later, Daniel Webster, from Massachusetts, rose in the Senate to speak. Mann had not anticipated that Webster would be willing to compromise the slavery issue: "He will have too much regard for his *historic* character and for his consistency to do any such thing; at least I hope so," he wrote to his wife.

But to the amazement and deep perturbation of Mann and other former admirers, Webster made an about-face and surrendered to the slave interests. The famous orator was making a bid for the presidency in the "Seventh of March" speech. His opening lines were: "I wish to speak today, not as a Massachusetts man, not as a Northern man, but as an American. I speak for the preservation of the Union." Webster damned "the infernal Fanatics and Abolitionists" who would override the Constitution, if they had the power, and defy the Supreme Court. It was the North's duty to return slaves who had escaped into the free states, he said—thus helping to pave the way for the infamous "Fugitive Slave Law," to be enacted later in the year.

As an example of great rhetoric, Mann considered Webster's speech, which lasted more than three hours, a masterpiece, characterized by "clearness of style, weight of statement, power of language, but nothing in my mind can atone for the abandonment of the territories to what he calls the law of nature, for the exclusions of slavery." Mann condemned Webster as a deserter from an army fighting for a great cause. To his wife, he wrote, "he is a fallen star! Lucifer descended from heaven! His intellectual life has been one great epic, and now he has given a vile catastrophe to its closing pages. He has walked for years among the gods, to descend from the empyrean heights, and mingle with mimes and apes! I am overwhelmed."

It was Horace Mann who, as Theodore Parker phrased it, "smote the champion of slavery a blow which sent him reeling home: it was the heaviest blow Webster ever had." And Charles Sumner noted that "Webster men" were conceding that "Horace Mann is a formidable antagonist." In a forty-page letter to Massachusetts voters, Mann was scathing in his criticism of Webster's conduct, quoting from Webster's own speeches to show that he had previously favored Free Soil and championed freedom; now he had deserted the principles he had formerly held and had gone directly contrary to the opinions of his constituents.

Webster was unaccustomed to such outspoken opposition. He swore vengeance against Mann, determining to prevent his reelection to Congress. As Mann described the situation, "Three fifths of all the Whig Presses went over in a day. The word of command went forth to annihilate me. . . .From having been complimented on all sides, I was misrepresented, maligned, travestied, on all sides. Not a single Whig paper in Boston defended me." Webster and his backers succeeded in blocking Mann's renomination by the Whigs in 1850, but the Free Soil Convention proceeded to give him its nomination. Mann was certain that he would be defeated, but after a strenuous campaign, in which he appealed to independent voters, a "handsome majority" (actually forty-one votes) turned out to reelect him for a third term. His bitter enemy, Daniel Webster, was appointed Secretary of State by Millard Fillmore, but was refused nomination for the presidency by the Whigs in 1852, and, frustrated and bitter, died a few months later.

Horace Mann's final speech in the House, delivered on February 28, 1851, was a lengthy attack on the legality and constitutionality of the Fugitive Slave Law. His manuscript, which he was able to present only in brief because of a five-minute gag rule imposed by the Speaker, contains more than 100 case citations, drawn from a variety of legal sources. Mann argued eloquently that the law violated the spirit and the letter of the Constitution. In a stirring passage, reminiscent of Patrick Henry, Mann concluded: "In the name of my constituents, and by the memory of that 'old man eloquent,' [John Quincy Adams] in whose place it is my fortune to stand, I demand it because it is a law which wars against the fundamental principles of human liberty and because it is a law which conflicts with the constitution of the country, and with all the judicial interpretations of that constitution, wherever they have been applied to the white race." A series of other "becauses" enumerated by Mann condemned the law as "abhorrent to the moral and religious sentiments of a vast majority of the community that is called upon to enforce it"; it made the free states "participators in the guilt of slaveholding;. . .it is a law which disgraces our country in the eyes of the whole civilized world"; and "it is a law which renders the precepts of the gospel and the teachings of Jesus Christ seditious."

A new factor was introduced into the situation later in the same year as Mann's last speech. An acute observation by Jonathan Messerli, in his biography of Mann, reads: "for all the tidal wave of words uttered by courageous angry men bent on destroying the Fugitive Slave Law in 1851, none of their efforts created anything like the powerful groundswell of moral indignation accomplished by a book from the pen of the obscure wife of a Bowdoin College professor, Harriet Beecher Stowe."[74] The first installment of *Uncle Tom's Cabin* appeared in the Washington, D.C., *National Era* on June 5, 1851. One of the immediate effects of the book was to make impossible the enforcement of the Fugitive Slave Law. Outside the South, noncooperation with the law was virtually unanimous. More ominous, the book whipped up an enormous volume of antislavery sentiment and perhaps made inevitable the outbreak of the Civil War.

In any event, Horace Mann's congressional career was coming to a close, and he was ready to turn to new fields of endeavor.

CHAPTER 14

Antioch Years

While Horace Mann was still a member of Congress, in March, 1852, he had been approached by a representative of a new Protestant sect, the "Christian Connexion," the members of which referred to themselves simply as "Christians," with a proposal that he come out to Ohio as president of a new college to be called Antioch. Mann was attracted by the offer, in part because it would provide an escape from the political turmoil in which he had been embroiled for the past five years, and, probably even more by the opportunity the position would give for experimentation in another field of education. Two other features of the college, as projected, appealed to him: it was to be nonsectarian and there would be no discrimination based on sex or race.

A year and a half earlier the Christian Connexion had taken preliminary steps to establish a college which would be representative of its faith. The sect's creed was based entirely upon the Bible. Evidence of a Christian life was the single criterion for membership. The name of the college was suggested by the words of Acts XI:26: "And the disciples were called Christians first in Antioch." Originally, the intention had been to locate the institution in upstate New York, but more generous financial support was pledged by a group of Ohio businessmen. The final decision was in favor of a village in southwestern Ohio, called Yellow Springs, some seventy-five miles northeast of Cincinnati. The little community of 400 inhabitants was famed for its medicinal springs—from which its name was taken—, the local scenery was delightful, and the climate was healthful.

Antioch's offer was pondered by Horace Mann for several months before acceptance. Close friends familiar with conditions in the western frontier area, to which Ohio then belonged, advised strongly against his going. A letter to Mann from Catherine Beecher, whose father had been president of the Lane Theological Seminary in Cincinnati, warned him that for students he could expect a "strange medley of raw, ignorant boys, not one tenth of whom will stay over a year and will go off unlamented," and further that the founder of any college west of the Alleghenies would experience a "legion of cares, perplexities, charges, and disappointments." Another close friend and valued counselor, Samuel Gridley Howe, was amazed that Mann would even consider the proposition, much less accept it.

Other aspects of the situation also discouraged Mann and caused him to lose interest: the responsibility for running the college was to be shared with the business manager, A. M. Merrifield; the promised presidential salary of $3,000 was reduced to $2,000; selection of a faculty was to be in the hands of a board of trustees, instead of the president's; and, worst of all, the financial prospects were extremely precarious. The college's endowment was to be created through a system of scholarships, sold for $100 each and entitling their owners to their use for one student *in perpetuity.* This strange scheme was destined to become a millstone; in effect, it meant that there would be fewer and fewer paying students.

In the interim, Mann was nominated for governor of Massachusetts as the Free Soil candidate. After a strenuous campaign, with the vote split several ways, the Whigs emerged with a plurality, and Horace Mann's political career came to an end. He blamed his defeat on rum and proslavery; a decisive factor, too, may have been the virulent opposition of Daniel Webster's followers. In any event, Mann now found himself out of accord with the political forces currently in power in the Commonwealth and decided that he had no political future in the state. By way of Antioch, he could return to his favorite field, education, and test some long-cherished educational ideas. The presidency of the college was accepted. Mann thus entered upon one of the most constructive, but at the same time perhaps the most tragic and frustrating stage of his life.

President Mann's first step was to call a faculty meeting at West Newton, Massachusetts, a group which included his niece and nephew, Rebecca and Calvin Pennell. The unanimity of views of the faculty on several matters important to Mann pleased him: "We were all teetotalers; all anti-tobacco men; all anti-slavery men; a majority of us believe in phrenology; all anti-emulation men, that is all against any system of rewards and prizes designed to withdraw the mind from a comparison of itself with a standard of excellence, and to substitute a rival for that standard. We agreed entirely as to religious and chapel exercises."

An early task was to develop a course of study for Antioch's students. The basic subjects were to be Latin, Greek, English, mathematics, history, and the natural sciences. Mann insisted that physiology and hygiene should also be required for every student. Elective courses offered the students included astronomy, geology, civil engineering, and political science. An alternative program without Greek or Latin led to the Bachelor of Arts degree. Scientific and historical studies were stressed to a greater extent than was common among colleges of the day. Since it was anticipated that many of the students would elect to become teachers, "the study of the theory and practice of teaching was made a part of the regular course, thus incorporating the work of preparing young persons to teach in the very organization of the college." So far as the record shows, this was the first appearance of the normal school idea in an American college.

As to methods of teaching, Mann proposed to discourage the excessive use of textbooks; teaching from books alone was compared by Mann to administering the same prescription to all the patients in a hospital. Instead, instruction was to be mainly oral, through lectures and individual conferences. Memorization for recitation purposes was ruled out. Mann himself assumed a heavy teaching load in addition to his other duties—all favorite subjects: political economy, intellectual and moral philosophy, constitutional law, and natural theology, giving him an opportunity to present his views on religion, morals, phrenology, and civil and governmental matters.

When Mann had agreed to go to Ohio, he had been promised that the college's physical plant would be in complete readiness for the announced opening date, in the fall of 1853. In the course of a lecture tour in the Middle West in December, 1852, a visit was paid to Yellow Springs. It was raining when Mann arrived and he stepped off the train into a sea of mud; nevertheless, the scenery impressed him and he could visualize a beautiful campus in the future. The main building at Antioch was in process of construction and Mann was assured that dormitories would be ready before the students arrived. He was disappointed to find that only stumps of great trees remained on the campus site, cleared to make way for the new buildings. In June, 1853, Mann wrote to inquire further about the progress of Antioch's buildings, and was again given assurances that all was well: plastering for the "female dormitory" was finished, the foundations for the "male dormitory" were laid, and materials were being procured for the president's house.

The grim realities were far different when the Mann family arrived in the fall. Buildings were incomplete and despite the promises that had been made, the president's house had not been started. Somewhat humorously, Mann remarked, "If Adam and Eve had been brought into this world as prematurely as we were brought on the premises of Antioch College, they must have been created about Wednesday night." There were no fences around the campus, halls had no doors, and it was not an uncommon sight to see pigs walking through the dining room. The space assigned to the library contained neither books nor shelves, while the classrooms lacked blackboards, desks, and chairs. A hydraulic pump, installed to pump water up from a spring to the campus level, broke down, and students had to use pitchers and pails to fill a water tower a quarter of a mile from their dormitory. A standard item of equipment for the students was a small wooden scraper to remove the mud from the bottoms of their shoes. Mann noted that "there was not a fireplace nor a stove in the whole establishment."

Undaunted by present and prospective future tribulations, Horace Mann prepared for inauguration day at Antioch, scheduled for October 5, 1853. Three thousand people streamed into Yellow Springs for the ceremony, arriving in wagons, carts, on horseback, and afoot. They were properly rewarded. For this great occasion, Horace Mann delivered the longest and most polished speech he ever made—requiring two hours for delivery and running to 27,000 words in the printed version. The history of civilization was reviewed to show the destiny of mankind and the moral capabilities of the human race. The infinite possibilities of the Mississippi Valley, both material and spiritual, were also fully perceived. In an era devoted to oratory and lengthy perorations, Horace Mann pulled out all the stops, with such passages as these:

And a youthful community or State is like a child. Its bones are in the gristle, and can be shaped into symmetry of form and nobleness of stature. Its heart overflows with generosity and hope, and its habits of thought have not yet been hardened into insoluble dogmatism. This youthful Western world is gigantic youth, and therefore its education must be such as befits a giant. It is born to such power as no heir to an earthly throne ever inherited, and it must be trained to make that power a blessing and not a curse to mankind. With its mighty frame stretching from the Alleghenies to the Rocky Mountains, and with great rivers for arteries to circulate its blood, it must have a sensorium to which all mighty interests of mankind can be mapped out; and in its colossal and Briarean form, there must be a heart large enough to swim in. Wherever the capital of the United States may be, this valley will be its seat of empire. No other valley—the Danube, the Ganges, the Nile or the Amazon—is ever to exert so formative an influence as this upon the destinies of men; and, therefore, in civil polity, in ethics, in studying and obeying the laws of God, it must ascend to a contemplation of a future and enduring reign of beneficence and peace.[75]

Mann remarked further that despite the notable achievements of scientists, inventors, and philosophers in the Western world, greed, injustice, and violence had continued to increase. Mankind, however, is perfectible, he maintained, and its mind, spirit and energies should now be turned toward creating a world free from war, poverty, disease, and political and religious persecution. To achieve such a millennium, great institutions of higher education were ideal instruments, and Mann pledged that Antioch would be dedicated to this high purpose.

After the president's inspiring and stirring address and the generally auspicious events of inauguration day, Mann and his faculty and students had to return to earth. Classrooms were unfinished, and therefore the tables in the dining room had to be cleared after breakfast for the college entrance examinations to begin. About 150 candidates appeared to take the written tests, spread over several days. It was a motley group, ranging in age from fourteen to forty, married and unmarried, some ministers who had given up their parishes to take a college course of study, a number of farmers' and mechanics' sons and daughters, and a few students from prominent Eastern families, attracted by Mann's reputation.

The examinations were difficult, and upon their completion, Mann was dismayed to discover that only two women and six men were qualified to enter the freshman class. Mary Mann wrote back to a Massachusetts friend, "I do not think you ever imagined the profundity of their ignorance. Many of these great *women* cannot read intelligibly. . . .Our college is in fact a school." Fortunately, a high school or preparatory division of Antioch was included in the advance planning and some 325 students were admitted to the preparatory school during the first year, 1853-54. Later, as applications for admission increased substantially in number, Mann was able to set higher standards for entering students.

The physical difficulties under which the faculty and students struggled during the initial period were little short of appalling. Many cold weeks elapsed before stoves arrived to heat either the main college building or the student dormitories. Professors had to move into their apartments in the college building before the plaster was dry and while it was still impossible to make a fire. The Manns' household effects were lost en route from the East and when finally delivered were found to have suffered extensive damage. Stools were used for seats, with chairs regarded as an excessive refinement.

A far greater peril was the financial situation. A. M. Merrifield, Antioch's business manager, had mismanaged the college's funds, and in effect the institution was bankrupt the day it opened. In the beginning, Mann paid little attention to finances, since he had no direct responsibility for that phase of the operation. When he awoke to the true state of affairs, he discovered that unpaid creditors were legion in number, that there was insufficient money to pay faculty salaries and none to cover payments due on the college mortgage. When bills for the college's impractical but expensive buildings came due, Merrifield used the scholarship funds, presumed to be for endowment, to satisfy the insurance company which held the mortgage. Although Mann's salary had been fixed at two thousand dollars a year, he never received more than half of that amount. The faculty, too, was on half pay or less. Professors who were ministers preached during school recesses and vacations to earn living expenses, and Mann went on extended lecture tours, earning $50 or more for each appearance.

The most critical year for Antioch came during the financial panic of 1857. Factories were closed, business and trade slumped, unemployment was widespread, runs were made on banks, and bankruptcies among corporations and individuals were epidemic. New blows were in store for the college, already beset by debt and dissension. A moving spirit in the enterprise, Judge William Mills, who had given liberally of his wealth to found the college, was driven into bankruptcy and his property was sold to satisfy his creditors, leaving the college with an unpaid pledge of thousands of dollars. A congressman in Antioch's district, who had pledged an even larger sum, lost practically everything and was unable to help. The student body decreased in size, partly because of lack of funds, partly because they had lost confidence in the institution's future.

The insurance company which held the mortgage on the college pressed for payment. When it became obvious that the institution was insolvent, on April 20, 1859, the grounds and equipment were sold in the U. S. Court in Cincinnati for about $40,000, a fraction of the indebtedness. Friends of Mann bought the college, reorganized it, and appointed a new board of trustees, who would be fiscally responsible and also free of the sectarianism which had been so troublesome to Mann in the past.

The most unfortunate aspect of the recurring financial woes, from Horace Mann's point of view, was that his time, energy, and mind were being diverted and dissipated from important educational goals. How could his great ambitions for Antioch be realized when the college's very existence was hanging in the balance? Nevertheless, a certain degree of progress was evident.

A feature of the Antioch scheme which had attracted Mann from the outset was that the college was to be coeducational, a radical departure from the conventional practices of the day. He found appealing the concept of a college which would provide an opportunity for "redressing the long-inflicted wrongs of woman by giving her equal advantages of education—with men," as he wrote to Eli Fay, chairman of a committee which helped to establish Antioch. Mann had stated, without equivocation, that if he went to Antioch he would appoint women as well as men to the faculty, for two reasons: they made excellent teachers, and female students needed maternal as well as paternal advice and counsel.

Mann had, in fact, always strongly supported the movement for improvements in the education of women and had friends like Catherine Beecher who were interested in "ladies' seminaries." He had urged the employment of more women teachers in the common schools of Massachusetts, and was influential in substantially increasing the number during his term as Secretary of the Board of Education. Two of the first three normal schools established by the Board were coeducational from the beginning, and one was for women. A precedent, too, was furnished by Oberlin College in Ohio, which was the first college in the country to be coeducational, starting in 1833, though most of the women at Oberlin took a course of study two years shorter than the regular curriculum. During lecture tours in western New York and Ohio, before assuming the Antioch presidency, Mann had found both men and women "far more interested in the subject of female education than they are in Massachusetts." Among the possible reasons for this phenomenon were a spirit of economy, since both sexes could be educated less expensively in one institution, and a stronger feeling of democracy existing in frontier areas.

Within Antioch, women met men on an equal footing. President Mann was a firm believer in equal education, but he did not argue for an identical education for men and women. His view was that a woman should be educated as a woman; she should not attempt to wear whiskers or sing bass. After five years of what Mann described as "our great experiment," he was convinced of the validity of coeducation: the mingling of the sexes, he maintained, was mutually advantageous, the young women refined the manners of the young men, and the young men provided "balance" for the women by eliminating "girlish romance" and the temptation to read novels. "Each sex has exercised a salutary influence over the other," Mann stated, for "they have stimulated each other intellectually and sustained each other morally."

Coeducation, while presenting many virtues also had its perils, as Mann was well aware. To a correspondent asking advice about starting a similar college, he wrote:

The advantages of a joint education are *very great*. The dangers of it are *terrible*. I have seen enough of young men to satisfy me, that in our present state of society there is not any great majority who would not yield to the temptation of ruining a girl if he could. The girls are far more pure but are they safe? We have never had here the happening of one of those events *mildly called accidents* but it is only because of our constant, sleepless vigilance.[76]

As one of his biographers, Louise Hall Tharp, observed, "Mann never ceased to be fearful lest his young men and maidens should tread not only the paths of the Glen together but the Primrose Path as well!" Seeking to provide a natural, wholesome environment, Mann gave the students, male and female, frequent opportunities to meet in evening gatherings and at other affairs in the presence of the teachers, to encourage general social intercourse but not individual dating. If coeducation was to succeed at Antioch, always in the eye of a critical public, no breath of scandal must touch the students. One of Mann's rules, accordingly, was that "Young Gentlemen and Ladies are not allowed to take walks or rides together unless accompanied by one of the teachers." The beautiful glen, across the railroad from the college, naturally attracted the students; it was ruled, however, that "in order to give the respective sexes opportunities of visiting the Glen, they will have the privilege to do so on alternate days only: the young Gentlemen may visit it on the odd days of each month, the young Ladies on the even days."

It is of interest to note that despite such handicaps and restrictions, engagements and weddings among the early students at Antioch were frequent occurrences.

Since his early days as Secretary of the Board of Education, Mann had been vitally concerned with problems of student discipline and punishment. Antioch provided him with a laboratory to test some of his theories. In Eastern colleges, student misbehavior was a chronic condition; town-and-gown riots and similar disorders were commonplace. Mann was determined that Antioch should become a model of good behavior. In dealing with the common schools, he had insisted that the harshness and severity of such discipline as corporal punishment could be replaced by other forms of control. Projecting his philosophy to the college level, he believed that if a greater degree of sympathy and confidence could be developed between students and faculty, better behavior would result and higher ideals be instilled. Mann made it a point to become personally acquainted with each student and he spent much time in private, intimate, and confidential conversations with individuals. The success of the method was attested to by the president as the college's second year began. The students, he noted, were "a most exemplary set of young people," because of which there was "obedience without punishment, order without espionage, great diligence without any trace of an artificial system of emulation." Mann resolved that no student guilty of immorality should ever receive the college's diploma, which he considered a certificate of character as well as of scholastic achievement.

To guide student conduct, thirty-one rules in a list of "Rules and Regulations" were posted; five more were added subsequently. Students were "prohibited from using tobacco on the college premises," which meant chewing tobacco, since cigarettes had not yet been invented. "Fire-arms and liquor" were also banned. Mann was so persuasive that by the end of the first year all except three students had given up tobacco, and these three were later expelled for drunkenness.

Second in seriousness only to Antioch's financial dilemma, among Mann's administrative problems, were the religious controversies which soon erupted, a bugbear which appears to have bedeviled him at every step in his career. Almost from the beginning of his presidency at Antioch, there had been some hostility to Mann because of his liberal religious views—an excuse used by conservatives to withhold gifts and repudiate pledges. A proposal to establish a theological department in the college was rejected by Mann on the ground that it would be in direct conflict with the nonsectarian principle on which the institution was founded. Soon after Mann and his family arrived at Antioch they became members of the local Christian Connexion church. A Bible class in the church was regularly taught by Mann and he began the college's day with prayers. Nevertheless, his advanced religious beliefs were anathema to many, being even less acceptable in Ohio than in his native Massachusetts. Inevitably, he came into conflict with the church leaders of various groups. Mann's well-meaning attempts to participate in the management of the local church were misunderstood and led to the formation of an anti-Mann faction in the town. The differences soon created dissension on the campus as well as outside the college. Certain trouble-making faculty members were discharged and there was disagreement in selecting replacements. Mann was charged with betraying the Christians and turning the college over to the Unitarians.

Not until Antioch was declared bankrupt and sold at auction to Mann's friends in 1859 did he win the war against the sectarians. A new liberal board of trustees assured him against further sectarian interference in the management of the college's affairs. But by then, Mann, worn out with the struggle against the myriad problems encountered during his six years as president, was rapidly nearing the end of his career.

A comparatively minor controversy, though important as an indication of Mann's character, simmered during his years at Antioch. This was the race issue. Antioch was the second college in Ohio to admit Negroes, being preceded only by Oberlin, which had pioneered in opening its doors to the colored race. Mary Mann, in her biography of her husband notes that "Mr. Mann's principle and resolution in regard to refusing admittance to no one on account of their color was a temporary disadvantage to the college, and alienated many who would otherwise have contributed to its support." Mrs. Mann could recall only two instances, however, of parents withdrawing their children from the college because of "the presence of two lovely young ladies of ·talent and refinement, who were slightly tinged in complexion."

Innovative in another respect was Mann's decision to eliminate honors and prizes—to him a long-held principle. His view was that children love knowledge and enjoy learning for its own sake and need no such artificial stimulant. When a friend in the East offered a gift to establish a prize at Antioch, Mann declined it.

The June, 1859, commencement at Antioch was Horace
Mann's last. The college had been saved and was now on a solid
foundation, ready to fulfill its mission. In a memorable bac-
calaureate address to the graduating class, his last public address,
Mann concluded with this farewell message:

So, in the infinitely nobler battle in which you are engaged against error
and wrong, if ever repulsed or stricken down, may you always be
solaced and cheered by the exulting cry of triumph over some abuse in
Church and State, some vice or folly in society, some false opinion or
cruelty or guilt which you have overcome! And I beseech you to treasure
up in your hearts these my parting words: *Be ashamed to die until you have
won some victory for humanity.* [77]

Immediately after the commencement exercises, Mann became seriously ill. He lingered through the summer months but
died the second day of August at the age of sixty-three, before he
could enjoy his hard-won success.

A long-time member of the Antioch faculty, Paul Bixler, writing some eighty years after Horace Mann's death, in reviewing
Mann's multifarious career concluded that "Antioch College is
today the most tangible heritage he left behind him, for it holds
more closely to his ideas than one might reasonably
expect. . . .His ideas at Antioch show a greater originality than
those of his Massachusetts career. He was more experienced in
education; he knew at last exactly where he wanted to go. Coeducation, the teaching of physiology and science, learning without
artificial stimulus or social restriction, symmetry, a strong moral
code—he took them all and against odds made them generally
effective." [78]

CHAPTER 15

Afterword

As an educational evangelist Horace Mann richly earned the reputation which later brought about his election to the Hall of Fame for Great Americans. The Massachusetts Board of Education in its *Twelfth Annual Report,* taking note of Mann's resignation as Secretary to enter Congress, expressed the consensus of his contemporaries: "We need not say that Mr. Mann has faithfully performed the duties of the office he has held, for twelve years, and thoroughly aroused the people of this Commonwealth to the importance of Common School education. He has devoted himself to this great work with a noble, self-denying zeal, and has enstamped his name so deeply on the educational interests of the State, that it will never be effaced"—a verdict to which later educators and historians are unlikely to take exception.

The concept of a comprehensive system of popular education did not originate with Mann. French philosophers during the Age of Reason held similar views, as a corollary of their belief in the perfectibility of the human race. In America, Thomas Jefferson and Benjamin Rush had advanced proposals of the same nature. The practical effects of such philosophical theories, however, were virtually nil. It remained for Mann to convince the leaders and masses of people that popular education possessed enormous potentials, a device that would provide equality of opportunity for all and become "the balance wheel of the social machinery." Without universal education, as Mann saw it, there would be revolution and a devastating breakdown of society. If the lower classes were allowed to suffer in ignorance, poverty, and misery, society as a whole would be imperiled by crime and violence.

To Mann, the free common school, whose beginning in Massachusetts dated back to the mid-seventeenth century, was the most fundamental discovery in the history of human progress. "Our means of education," he declared, "are the grand machinery by which the 'raw material' of human nature can be worked up into inventors and discoverers, into skilled artisans and scientific farmers, into scholars and jurists, into the founders of benevolent institutions."[79]

Mann looked upon children at birth as completely pliable organisms, neither good nor bad, but each one, almost without exception, capable of being shaped into useful and creative careers. In 1847, to substantiate this conviction and his unqualified faith in education, Mann sent out a circular and questionnaire to a number of experienced teachers posing the question: "What proportion or percentage of those under your own care . . . could be turned out the blessing, and not the bane, the honor, and not the scandal, of society? How much of improvement, in the upright conduct and good morals of the community, might we reasonably hope and expect, if all our Common Schools were what they should be?" The responses to Mann's hypothetical questions were remarkably unanimous. The teachers were certain that virtually all children could be trained to become good and useful citizens. A typical answer was that there were "scarcely one or two percent of really incorrigible members that the common schools could not mold."

The material achievements in Massachusetts schools during Mann's time were notable. Under his direction and stimulus, impressive gains had been scored. Taxes for school support had been raised and small, inefficient school districts had been consolidated into larger units. Private schools, which had previously received seventy-five percent of the educational funds were cut back to thirty-six percent of the total cost of schools. When Mann became Secretary, the average annual salary for men teachers in elementary schools was $185, for women $65; during his tenure, salaries for men rose by sixty-two percent, for women by fifty-four percent. Professional standards for teachers were raised in the newly established normal schools, teachers' institutes, and annual county educational conventions. At the beginning of the period, one-third of the state's children were not enrolled in school and school terms for others were short, averaging only two or three months; within two years a minimum year of six months had been established. The appropriation for public education was doubled and two million dollars obtained for better schoolhouses and equipment.

Such reforms and improvements could hardly have been accomplished by Mann singlehanded. An aroused public opinion and strong legislative support were key factors. Mann's own contributions, however, were of inestimable importance and influence, notably: his annual reports, which disseminated knowledge and information about existing conditions and needed reforms; his editing of the semimonthly *Common School Journal* for ten years, 1838-1848, supplementing the series of reports; and his remarkable talents as a public speaker before a variety of organizations, during which he sought to stimulate and educate public opinion about the purpose, value, and needs of public education. In sum, he was a powerful persuader.

"Above all," as Kathleen Edgerton Kendall expressed it, Mann "appealed to the moral, political, and economic desires of nineteenth-century Massachusetts. Citizens had the opportunity to choose good instead of evil, safety for republican institutions instead of chaotic mob rule, and business prosperity instead of insecurity."[80]

Mann's wide vision and the broad scope of his interests are demonstrated by a listing of some of the major problems which absorbed his time and attention, during his term as Secretary of the Board of Education. At his urging, pupils were grouped into classes; compulsory school attendance was advocated; a system of school registers were inaugurated; better school supervision became accepted practice; the district school system was gradually being abolished in favor of larger administrative units; school funds were apportioned on the basis of the average attendance of pupils; high schools which had been abandoned were reestablished; legislation was enacted to establish school libraries; the school term was lengthened; school conventions were arranged for patrons and friends of education; the employment of women in the elementary grades was encouraged; uniform textbooks were adopted; and state aid was provided for all schools.

Equally significant were Mann's contributions to classroom methods and school management. Both oral and written composition were advocated by him; he strongly supported the word method in teaching reading; he urged the use of laboratory apparatus in teaching science; he favored the inductive as opposed to the dogmatic textbook teaching method; he believed that the emotions as well as the intellect should be educated; he held that pupils should be taught to think; he introduced school music in the elementary grades; and he opposed emulation and fear to force pupils to study. Excessive corporal punishment was condemned and kindness and love recommended as alternatives. "As a moral act," Mann wrote, "blind obedience is without value. As a moral act, also, obedience through fear is without value," adding, "A reform in character may be begun in fear, but if it ends in fear, it will prove to be no reform." An important psychological principle was recognized by Mann in discussing the relationship of success in school work to the mental health of pupils; he notes that failure "depresses the spirits, takes away all the animation and strength derived from hope, and utterly destroys the *ideal* of intellectual accuracy." A child learns, Mann emphasized, only when his interest is aroused, at which point he learns by his own desire.

The main theme in Mann's writings on educational subjects is universal education, free from any political or sectarian bias. Because of his controversies with the conservative clergy, it has often been charged, or assumed, that he opposed religious teaching in the public schools. The assumption is erroneous. Mann believed that morality must be based upon religion and that "no community will ever be religious without religious education." But sectarianism must be avoided. As viewed by Mann, "The religious education which a child receives at school, is not imparted to him, for the purpose of making him join this or that denomination, when he arrives at years of discretion, but for the purpose of enabling him to judge for himself according to the dictates of his own reason and conscience what his religious obligations are, and whither they lead."

Similarly, Mann resisted use of the schools for political propaganda and indoctrination. The fundamental principles of republican government and the nature of government should be taught. "The tempest of political strife" ought not to be released, and "all indoctrination into matters of controversy between hostile political parties is to be elsewhere sought for, and elsewhere imparted."

A better understanding of Mann's educational and social philosophy may be gained by observing that soon after his election as Secretary of the Board of Education he became converted to the doctrines of phrenology. This system of psychology, philosophy, and ethics, later largely discredited, attracted many of the intellectual leaders and prominent physicians of the period. The foremost representative of the new "science," George Combe, a Scotsman, became one of Mann's intimate friends, and his *The Constitution of Man* was characterized by Mann as the "greatest book that has been written for centuries." In a recent history of the movement, John D. Davies writes that Mann "regarded phrenology as the greatest discovery of the ages and built all his theories of mental and moral improvement upon the ideas which it had furnished him."[81]

Prior to the development of modern psychology, phrenology was the experimental psychology of its day. Its chief bases were that the faculties of the human mind can be localized in the human brain and that the protuberances of the human skull indicate the location of these faculties. The philosophical and religious ideas preached by phrenologists were not original with them, including such doctrines as the perfectibility of man, the goodness of all nature, the reasonableness of religion, and the universal efficacy of science and its methods, but as the movement swept the land, the popularity of these notions for the salvation of the race spread widely. The aspect of phrenology which most fascinated Horace Mann was the extensive system of education built upon its teachings. The heart of the doctrine was that man is subject to definite laws of nature; by using his intelligence and by cooperating with science man could avoid all physical and moral evil simply by obedience to these laws. Here Horace Mann found support for his belief in universal education, especially training in the proper laws of health and morals.

Accordingly, he was convinced that the body as well as the soul must receive care; physical health is essential to efficiency, usefulness, and happiness; food and clothing, as well as books, studies, schools, and sermons are moral factors; environment is of great importance in human development; and the race can be improved by conscious effort.

Horace Mann was not a philosopher, theorist, or scientific pedagogue. In everything that he undertook, he looked for the practical and the useful. His practical talents explain his success in, for example, the improvement of the Massachusetts public schools. As a man of action, with no philosophical bent, his approach to all problems was strictly pragmatic: will it work, can it be made effective? His leaning toward the utilitarian sometimes led him to extremes, as for instance in thinking that children should study bookkeeping instead of algebra, because one would be of use and not the other, and country children should study surveying instead of geometry in order to be able to measure land and lay out roads.

Mann espoused many causes in a crowded and many-sided lifetime. His enduring place in American history, however, rests upon his notable services to public education. His influence was national and international. His efforts, combined with those of other educational pioneers, inaugurated a period so marked by educational progress and reform that it is now recognized as the era of the common school revival in the United States.

Notes and References

1. Mann, Mary Peabody, *Life of Horace Mann*. Boston: Walker, Fuller, 1865, p. 13.
2. Mann, Mary Peabody, *op. cit.*, pp. 11-12.
3. Mann, Mary Peabody, *op. cit.*, p. 13.
4. Mann, Mary Peabody, *op. cit.*, p. 12.
5. Messerli, Jonathan, *Horace Mann, a Biography*. N.Y.: Alfred A. Knopf, 1972, pp. 31-32.
6. Messerli, *op. cit.*, p. 123.
7. Messerli, *op. cit.*, pp. 135-36.
8. Mann, Mary Peabody, *op. cit.*, p. 70.
9. Mann, Mary Peabody, *op. cit.*, pp. 80-81.
10. Mann, Horace, *Twelfth Annual Report*, 1848, p. 17.
11. Mann, Horace, *Second Annual Report*, 1838, pp. 27-28.
12. Mann, Horace, *Horace Mann on the Crisis in Education*. Yellow Springs, Ohio: Antioch College Press, 1965, pp. 100-101.
13. Hinsdale, B. A., *Horace Mann*. N.Y.: Scribner, 1913, p. 4.
14. Hinsdale, *op. cit.*, p. 16.
15. Mann, Horace, *Tenth Annual Report*, 1846, p. 230.
16. Odell, William R., "Finding and Developing Leadership Today for America's Public Schools," *Educational Forum*, 23 (March, 1958), p. 339.
17. Mann, Horace, *First Annual Report*, 1837, p. 58.
18. Mann, Horace, *First Annual Report*, 1837, p. 59.
19. Mann, Horace, *First Annual Report*, 1837, pp. 27-28.
20. Mann, Horace, *Fifth Annual Report*, 1841, p. 38.
21. Mann, Horace, *Fourth Annual Report*, 1840, pp. 48-60.
22. Mann, Horace, *Fourth Annual Report*, 1840, pp. 49-50.
23. Mann, Horace, *Second Annual Report*, 1838, pp. 44-45.
24. Mann, Horace, *Eleventh Annual Report*, 1847, pp. 94-95.
25. Mann, Horace, *Eleventh Annual Report*, 1847, p. 96.
26. Mann, Horace, *Eleventh Annual Report*, 1847, p. 97.
27. Mann, Horace, *Sixth Annual Report*, 1842, pp. 32-35.

28. *Common School Journal*, 5 (1843), p. 65.
29. Williams, E. I. F., *Horace Mann, Educational Statesman* N.Y.: Macmillan, 1937, pp. 194-95.
30. Mann, Horace, *First Annual Report*, 1837, pp. 11-12.
31. Barnard, Henry, *American Journal of Education*, Dec., 1858, pp. 638-39.
32. Mann, Horace, *Twelfth Annual Report*, 1848, pp. 27-28.
33. Mann, Horace, *First Annual Report*, 1837, p. 34.
34. Mann, Horace, *Second Annual Report*, 1838, pp. 62-63.
35. Mann, Horace, *Second Annual Report*, 1838, p. 68.
36. Mann, Horace, *Second Annual Report*, 1838, p. 78.
37. Mann, Horace, *Fifth Annual Report*, 1841, p. 37.
38. Mann, Horace, *Third Annual Report*, 1839, pp. 24-36, 47-100.
39. Mann, Horace, *Third Annual Report*, 1839, pp. 57-58.
40. Mann, Horace, *Third Annual Report*, 1839, p. 60.
41. Mann, Horace, *Third Annual Report*, 1839, p. 24.
42. Hinsdale, *op. cit.*, p. 135.
43. Mann, Horace, *Third Annual Report*, 1839, p. 39.
44. Mann, Horace, *Sixth Annual Report*, 1842, p. 66.
45. Mann, Horace, *Sixth Annual Report*, 1842, p. 160.
46. McClusky, Neil Gerard, *Public Schools and Moral Education*. N.Y.: Columbia Univ. Press, 1958, p. 70
47. Culver, Raymond B., *Horace Mann and Religion in the Massachusetts Public Schools*. New Haven: Yale Univ. Press, 1929, pp. 205-206.
48. Messerli, *op. cit.*, pp. 411-12.
49. McCluskey, *op. cit.*, p. 94.
50. Mann, Horace, *Twelfth Annual Report*, 1848, p. 140.
51. Mann, Horace, *Twelfth Annual Report*, 1848, p. 123.
52. Mann, Horace, *Seventh Annual Report*, 1843, p. 4.
53. Mann, Horace, *Seventh Annual Report*, 1843, p. 62.
54. Mann, Horace, *Seventh Annual Report*, 1843, p. 106.
55. Mann, Horace, *Seventh Annual Report*, 1843, p. 133.
56. Mann, Horace, *Seventh Annual Report*, 1843, p. 137.
57. Mann, Horace, *Seventh Annual Report*, 1843, p. 155.
58. Mann, Horace, *Seventh Annual Report*, 1843, p. 138.
59. Mann, Horace, *Fifth Annual Report*, 1841, pp. 57-58.
60. Drake, William E., "Wanted: More Men Like Horace Mann," *School and Society*, 59 (April, 1944), p. 226.
61. Mann, Horace, *Third Annual Report*, 1839, p. 43.
62. Mann, Horace, *Eleventh Annual Report*, 1847, p. 109.
63. Mann, Horace, *Eleventh Annual Report*, 1847, p. 113.
64. Mann, Horace, *Fifth Annual Report*, 1841, p. 84
65. Mann, Horace, *Fifth Annual Report*, 1841, pp. 86-100.

66. Mann, Horace, *Twelfth Annual Report,* 1848, pp. 65-66.

67. Mann, Horace, *Twelfth Annual Report,* 1848, pp. 67-68.

68. Knight, Edgar W., "Some Evidence of Horace Mann's Influence in the South," *School and Society,* 65 (Jan. 18, 1947), pp. 33-37, and "More Evidence of Horace Mann's Influence in the South," *Educational Forum,* 12 (Jan., 1948), pp. 167-84.

69. Correas, Edmundo, "Sarmiento, the Educator," *Américas,* 16 (August, 1964), pp. 27-32; Ewing, Enrique E., "Centenary of a Friendship," *Bulletin of the Pan American Union,* 81 (Dec., 1947), pp. 664-67; French, William Marshall, "Horace Mann and Education Abroad," *School and Society,* 88 (April 9, 1960), pp. 186-88; King, Clyde S., "Horace Mann's Influence on South American Libraries," *History of Education Quarterly,* 1 (Dec., 1961), pp. 16-26; Miller, J. Hillis, "Horace Mann and Latin American Education," *School and Society,* 71 (April 8, 1950), pp. 211-13.

70. Compayré, Gabriel, *Horace Mann and the Public School in the United States.* N.Y.: Thomas Y. Crowell, 1907, p. 132.

71. Mann, Horace, "Speech Delivered in the House of Representatives," February 28, 1851, in: Mann, Horace, *Slavery, Letters and Speeches.* Boston, 1851, pp 390-91.

72. Mann, Horace, "Speech Delivered in the House of Representatives," February 15, 1850, in: Mann, Horace, *Slavery, Letters and Speeches.* Boston, 1851, p. 216.

73. Mann, Horace, "Speech Delivered in the House of Representatives," February 23, 1849, in: Mann, Horace, *Slavery, Letters and Speeches.* Boston, 1851, p. 216.

74. Messerli, *op. cit.,* p. 529.

75. Hinsdale, *op. cit.,* p. 246.

76. Tharp, Louise Hall, *Until Victory: Horace Mann and Mary Peabody.* Boston: Little, Brown, 1943, p. 281.

77. Mann, Horace, *Horace Mann on the Crisis in Education,* p. 243.

78. Bixler, Paul, "Horace Mann—Mustard Seed," *American Scholar,* 7 (Winter, 1938), pp. 36-38.

79. Mann, Horace, *Life and Works.* Boston, 1891, v. 4, p. 228.

80. Kendall, Kathleen Edgerton, "Education as 'the Balance Wheel of Social Machinery': Horace Mann's Arguments and Proofs." *Quarterly Journal of Speech,* 54 (Feb., 1968), p. 21.

81. Davies, John D., *Phrenology: Fad and Science, a 19th Century American Crusade.* New Haven: Yale Univ. Press, 1955, p. 85.

Selected Bibliography

COMPAYRÉ, GABRIEL. *Horace Mann and the Public School in the United States.* N. Y.: Crowell, 1907. 134 pp.

CULVER, RAYMOND BENJAMIN. *Horace Mann and Religion in the Massachusetts Public Schools.* New Haven: Yale Univ. Press, 1929. 301 pp.

HINSDALE, BURKE AARON. *Horace Mann and the Common School Revival in the United States.* N. Y.: Scribner, 1898. 326 pp.

HUBBELL, G.A. *Horace Mann in Ohio: a Study of the Application of His Public School Ideas to College Administration.* N. Y.: Columbia University, 1900. 70 pp.

KING, CLYDE S. *Horace Mann, 1796-1859; a Bibliography.* Dobbs Ferry, N. Y.: Oceana Publications, 1966. 453 pp.

MANN, HORACE. *Life and Works of Horace Mann* Ed. by Mary Mann. Boston: Walker, Fuller, 1865-68. 3 v. New and enlarged edition, Boston: Lee and Shepard, 1891. 5 v.

MANN, HORACE. *Massachusetts Board of Education, Annual Report,* 1-12. 1837-48. Boston, 1838-52. 12 v.

MANN, HORACE. *The Republic and the School; the Education of Free Men.* N. Y.: Teachers College, Columbia Univ., 1957. 112 pp.

MANN, HORACE. *Slavery: Letters and Speeches.* N.Y.: B. Franklin, 1969. 564 pp. (Reprint of 1851 edition.)

MANN, MARY TYLER (PEABODY), *Life of Horace Mann* New ed. Boston: W. Small, 1888, 609 pp.

MESSERLI, JONATHAN. *Horace Mann, a Biography.* N. Y.: Alfred A. Knopf, 1972. 604+xxxvii pp.

MORGAN, JOY ELMER. *Horace Mann, His Ideas and Ideals.* Washington, D.C.: National Home Library Foundation, 1936. 150 pp.

THARP, LOUISE HALL. *Until Victory: Horace Mann and Mary Peabody.* Boston: Little Brown, 1953. 367 pp.

WILLIAMS, EDWARD I. F. *Horace Mann, Educational Statesman.* N. Y.: Macmillan, 1937. 367 pp.

Index